C-4987   CAREER EXAMINATION SERIES

This is your
PASSBOOK for...

Stationary Engineer Apprentice

Test Preparation Study Guide
Questions & Answers

NLC®

NATIONAL LEARNING CORPORATION®

COPYRIGHT NOTICE

This book is SOLELY intended for, is sold ONLY to, and its use is RESTRICTED to individual, bona fide applicants or candidates who qualify by virtue of having seriously filed applications for appropriate license, certificate, professional and/or promotional advancement, higher school matriculation, scholarship, or other legitimate requirements of education and/or governmental authorities.

This book is NOT intended for use, class instruction, tutoring, training, duplication, copying, reprinting, excerption, or adaptation, etc., by:

1) Other publishers
2) Proprietors and/or Instructors of "Coaching" and/or Preparatory Courses
3) Personnel and/or Training Divisions of commercial, industrial, and governmental organizations
4) Schools, colleges, or universities and/or their departments and staffs, including teachers and other personnel
5) Testing Agencies or Bureaus
6) Study groups which seek by the purchase of a single volume to copy and/or duplicate and/or adapt this material for use by the group as a whole without having purchased individual volumes for each of the members of the group
7) Et al.

Such persons would be in violation of appropriate Federal and State statutes.

PROVISION OF LICENSING AGREEMENTS – Recognized educational, commercial, industrial, and governmental institutions and organizations, and others legitimately engaged in educational pursuits, including training, testing, and measurement activities, may address request for a licensing agreement to the copyright owners, who will determine whether, and under what conditions, including fees and charges, the materials in this book may be used them. In other words, a licensing facility exists for the legitimate use of the material in this book on other than an individual basis. However, it is asseverated and affirmed here that the material in this book CANNOT be used without the receipt of the express permission of such a licensing agreement from the Publishers. Inquiries re licensing should be addressed to the company, attention rights and permissions department.

All rights reserved, including the right of reproduction in whole or in part, in any form or by any means, electronic or mechanical, including photocopying, recording, or by any information storage and retrieval system, without permission in writing from the Publisher.

Copyright © 2024 by
National Learning Corporation

212 Michael Drive, Syosset, NY 11791
(516) 921-8888 • www.passbooks.com
E-mail: info@passbooks.com

PUBLISHED IN THE UNITED STATES OF AMERICA

PASSBOOK® SERIES

THE *PASSBOOK® SERIES* has been created to prepare applicants and candidates for the ultimate academic battlefield – the examination room.

At some time in our lives, each and every one of us may be required to take an examination – for validation, matriculation, admission, qualification, registration, certification, or licensure.

Based on the assumption that every applicant or candidate has met the basic formal educational standards, has taken the required number of courses, and read the necessary texts, the *PASSBOOK® SERIES* furnishes the one special preparation which may assure passing with confidence, instead of failing with insecurity. Examination questions – together with answers – are furnished as the basic vehicle for study so that the mysteries of the examination and its compounding difficulties may be eliminated or diminished by a sure method.

This book is meant to help you pass your examination provided that you qualify and are serious in your objective.

The entire field is reviewed through the huge store of content information which is succinctly presented through a provocative and challenging approach – the question-and-answer method.

A climate of success is established by furnishing the correct answers at the end of each test.

You soon learn to recognize types of questions, forms of questions, and patterns of questioning. You may even begin to anticipate expected outcomes.

You perceive that many questions are repeated or adapted so that you can gain acute insights, which may enable you to score many sure points.

You learn how to confront new questions, or types of questions, and to attack them confidently and work out the correct answers.

You note objectives and emphases, and recognize pitfalls and dangers, so that you may make positive educational adjustments.

Moreover, you are kept fully informed in relation to new concepts, methods, practices, and directions in the field.

You discover that you are actually taking the examination all the time: you are preparing for the examination by "taking" an examination, not by reading extraneous and/or supererogatory textbooks.

In short, this PASSBOOK®, used directedly, should be an important factor in helping you to pass your test.

STATIONARY ENGINEER APPRENTICE

DUTIES
Receives on-the-job training in becoming a Stationary/Operating Engineer. Performs related duties.

RESPONSIBILITIES
Responsibilities include, but are not limited to:
- Working rotating shifts including weekends and holidays.
- Climbing stairs, ladders and other means to access boiler room equipment, sometimes in confined spaces (e.g. accessing steam drums and fire boxes) or heating and ventilating rooms (e.g. air handlers and plenums) which may be dusty and dark with varying degrees of extreme temperatures.
- Standing upright for extended periods of time.
- Using vision to read small numbers and/or markings on gauges and equipment.
- Using vision and hearing to avoid injury from overhead piping and rotating machinery.
- Communicating orally in noisy working conditions.
- Working in areas containing gases from the combustion process and strong odors from grease, lubricants or solvents.
- Lifting heavy metal objects.
- Working with alkaline and acidic chemicals used in boiler water treatment and handling chemicals.
- Walking over wet and slippery surfaces.
- Working around hazardous materials, such as asbestos and infectious waste.
- Wearing personal protective equipment including but not limited to respirators, face shield and hearing protection.

SCOPE OF THE EXAMINATION
Candidates will be scheduled to take a comprehensive math exam and must score at least 85% out of 100% on the exam.

HOW TO TAKE A TEST

I. YOU MUST PASS AN EXAMINATION

A. WHAT EVERY CANDIDATE SHOULD KNOW

Examination applicants often ask us for help in preparing for the written test. What can I study in advance? What kinds of questions will be asked? How will the test be given? How will the papers be graded?

As an applicant for a civil service examination, you may be wondering about some of these things. Our purpose here is to suggest effective methods of advance study and to describe civil service examinations.

Your chances for success on this examination can be increased if you know how to prepare. Those "pre-examination jitters" can be reduced if you know what to expect. You can even experience an adventure in good citizenship if you know why civil service exams are given.

B. WHY ARE CIVIL SERVICE EXAMINATIONS GIVEN?

Civil service examinations are important to you in two ways. As a citizen, you want public jobs filled by employees who know how to do their work. As a job seeker, you want a fair chance to compete for that job on an equal footing with other candidates. The best-known means of accomplishing this two-fold goal is the competitive examination.

Exams are widely publicized throughout the nation. They may be administered for jobs in federal, state, city, municipal, town or village governments or agencies.

Any citizen may apply, with some limitations, such as the age or residence of applicants. Your experience and education may be reviewed to see whether you meet the requirements for the particular examination. When these requirements exist, they are reasonable and applied consistently to all applicants. Thus, a competitive examination may cause you some uneasiness now, but it is your privilege and safeguard.

C. HOW ARE CIVIL SERVICE EXAMS DEVELOPED?

Examinations are carefully written by trained technicians who are specialists in the field known as "psychological measurement," in consultation with recognized authorities in the field of work that the test will cover. These experts recommend the subject matter areas or skills to be tested; only those knowledges or skills important to your success on the job are included. The most reliable books and source materials available are used as references. Together, the experts and technicians judge the difficulty level of the questions.

Test technicians know how to phrase questions so that the problem is clearly stated. Their ethics do not permit "trick" or "catch" questions. Questions may have been tried out on sample groups, or subjected to statistical analysis, to determine their usefulness.

Written tests are often used in combination with performance tests, ratings of training and experience, and oral interviews. All of these measures combine to form the best-known means of finding the right person for the right job.

II. HOW TO PASS THE WRITTEN TEST

A. NATURE OF THE EXAMINATION

To prepare intelligently for civil service examinations, you should know how they differ from school examinations you have taken. In school you were assigned certain definite pages to read or subjects to cover. The examination questions were quite detailed and usually emphasized memory. Civil service exams, on the other hand, try to discover your present ability to perform the duties of a position, plus your potentiality to learn these duties. In other words, a civil service exam attempts to predict how successful you will be. Questions cover such a broad area that they cannot be as minute and detailed as school exam questions.

In the public service similar kinds of work, or positions, are grouped together in one "class." This process is known as *position-classification*. All the positions in a class are paid according to the salary range for that class. One class title covers all of these positions, and they are all tested by the same examination.

B. FOUR BASIC STEPS

1) Study the announcement

How, then, can you know what subjects to study? Our best answer is: "Learn as much as possible about the class of positions for which you've applied." The exam will test the knowledge, skills and abilities needed to do the work.

Your most valuable source of information about the position you want is the official exam announcement. This announcement lists the training and experience qualifications. Check these standards and apply only if you come reasonably close to meeting them.

The brief description of the position in the examination announcement offers some clues to the subjects which will be tested. Think about the job itself. Review the duties in your mind. Can you perform them, or are there some in which you are rusty? Fill in the blank spots in your preparation.

Many jurisdictions preview the written test in the exam announcement by including a section called "Knowledge and Abilities Required," "Scope of the Examination," or some similar heading. Here you will find out specifically what fields will be tested.

2) Review your own background

Once you learn in general what the position is all about, and what you need to know to do the work, ask yourself which subjects you already know fairly well and which need improvement. You may wonder whether to concentrate on improving your strong areas or on building some background in your fields of weakness. When the announcement has specified "some knowledge" or "considerable knowledge," or has used adjectives like "beginning principles of…" or "advanced … methods," you can get a clue as to the number and difficulty of questions to be asked in any given field. More questions, and hence broader coverage, would be included for those subjects which are more important in the work. Now weigh your strengths and weaknesses against the job requirements and prepare accordingly.

3) Determine the level of the position

Another way to tell how intensively you should prepare is to understand the level of the job for which you are applying. Is it the entering level? In other words, is this the position in which beginners in a field of work are hired? Or is it an intermediate or advanced level? Sometimes this is indicated by such words as "Junior" or "Senior" in the class title. Other jurisdictions use Roman numerals to designate the level – Clerk I, Clerk II, for example. The word "Supervisor" sometimes appears in the title. If the level is not indicated by the title, check the description of duties. Will you be working under very close supervision, or will you have responsibility for independent decisions in this work?

4) Choose appropriate study materials

Now that you know the subjects to be examined and the relative amount of each subject to be covered, you can choose suitable study materials. For beginning level jobs, or even advanced ones, if you have a pronounced weakness in some aspect of your training, read a modern, standard textbook in that field. Be sure it is up to date and has general coverage. Such books are normally available at your library, and the librarian will be glad to help you locate one. For entry-level positions, questions of appropriate difficulty are chosen -- neither highly advanced questions, nor those too simple. Such questions require careful thought but not advanced training.

If the position for which you are applying is technical or advanced, you will read more advanced, specialized material. If you are already familiar with the basic principles of your field, elementary textbooks would waste your time. Concentrate on advanced textbooks and technical periodicals. Think through the concepts and review difficult problems in your field.

These are all general sources. You can get more ideas on your own initiative, following these leads. For example, training manuals and publications of the government agency which employs workers in your field can be useful, particularly for technical and professional positions. A letter or visit to the government department involved may result in more specific study suggestions, and certainly will provide you with a more definite idea of the exact nature of the position you are seeking.

III. KINDS OF TESTS

Tests are used for purposes other than measuring knowledge and ability to perform specified duties. For some positions, it is equally important to test ability to make adjustments to new situations or to profit from training. In others, basic mental abilities not dependent on information are essential. Questions which test these things may not appear as pertinent to the duties of the position as those which test for knowledge and information. Yet they are often highly important parts of a fair examination. For very general questions, it is almost impossible to help you direct your study efforts. What we can do is to point out some of the more common of these general abilities needed in public service positions and describe some typical questions.

1) General information

Broad, general information has been found useful for predicting job success in some kinds of work. This is tested in a variety of ways, from vocabulary lists to questions about current events. Basic background in some field of work, such as sociology or economics, may be sampled in a group of questions. Often these are principles which have become familiar to most persons through exposure rather than through formal training. It is difficult to advise you how to study for these questions; being alert to the world around you is our best suggestion.

2) Verbal ability

An example of an ability needed in many positions is verbal or language ability. Verbal ability is, in brief, the ability to use and understand words. Vocabulary and grammar tests are typical measures of this ability. Reading comprehension or paragraph interpretation questions are common in many kinds of civil service tests. You are given a paragraph of written material and asked to find its central meaning.

3) Numerical ability

Number skills can be tested by the familiar arithmetic problem, by checking paired lists of numbers to see which are alike and which are different, or by interpreting charts and graphs. In the latter test, a graph may be printed in the test booklet which you are asked to use as the basis for answering questions.

4) Observation

A popular test for law-enforcement positions is the observation test. A picture is shown to you for several minutes, then taken away. Questions about the picture test your ability to observe both details and larger elements.

5) Following directions

In many positions in the public service, the employee must be able to carry out written instructions dependably and accurately. You may be given a chart with several columns, each column listing a variety of information. The questions require you to carry out directions involving the information given in the chart.

6) Skills and aptitudes

Performance tests effectively measure some manual skills and aptitudes. When the skill is one in which you are trained, such as typing or shorthand, you can practice. These tests are often very much like those given in business school or high school courses. For many of the other skills and aptitudes, however, no short-time preparation can be made. Skills and abilities natural to you or that you have developed throughout your lifetime are being tested.

Many of the general questions just described provide all the data needed to answer the questions and ask you to use your reasoning ability to find the answers. Your best preparation for these tests, as well as for tests of facts and ideas, is to be at your physical and mental best. You, no doubt, have your own methods of getting into an exam-taking mood and keeping "in shape." The next section lists some ideas on this subject.

IV. KINDS OF QUESTIONS

Only rarely is the "essay" question, which you answer in narrative form, used in civil service tests. Civil service tests are usually of the short-answer type. Full instructions for answering these questions will be given to you at the examination. But in case this is your first experience with short-answer questions and separate answer sheets, here is what you need to know:

1) **Multiple-choice Questions**

Most popular of the short-answer questions is the "multiple choice" or "best answer" question. It can be used, for example, to test for factual knowledge, ability to solve problems or judgment in meeting situations found at work.

A multiple-choice question is normally one of three types—
- It can begin with an incomplete statement followed by several possible endings. You are to find the one ending which *best* completes the statement, although some of the others may not be entirely wrong.
- It can also be a complete statement in the form of a question which is answered by choosing one of the statements listed.

- It can be in the form of a problem – again you select the best answer.

Here is an example of a multiple-choice question with a discussion which should give you some clues as to the method for choosing the right answer:

When an employee has a complaint about his assignment, the action which will *best* help him overcome his difficulty is to
- A. discuss his difficulty with his coworkers
- B. take the problem to the head of the organization
- C. take the problem to the person who gave him the assignment
- D. say nothing to anyone about his complaint

In answering this question, you should study each of the choices to find which is best. Consider choice "A" – Certainly an employee may discuss his complaint with fellow employees, but no change or improvement can result, and the complaint remains unresolved. Choice "B" is a poor choice since the head of the organization probably does not know what assignment you have been given, and taking your problem to him is known as "going over the head" of the supervisor. The supervisor, or person who made the assignment, is the person who can clarify it or correct any injustice. Choice "C" is, therefore, correct. To say nothing, as in choice "D," is unwise. Supervisors have and interest in knowing the problems employees are facing, and the employee is seeking a solution to his problem.

2) True/False Questions

The "true/false" or "right/wrong" form of question is sometimes used. Here a complete statement is given. Your job is to decide whether the statement is right or wrong.

SAMPLE: A roaming cell-phone call to a nearby city costs less than a non-roaming call to a distant city.

This statement is wrong, or false, since roaming calls are more expensive.

This is not a complete list of all possible question forms, although most of the others are variations of these common types. You will always get complete directions for answering questions. Be sure you understand *how* to mark your answers – ask questions until you do.

V. RECORDING YOUR ANSWERS

Computer terminals are used more and more today for many different kinds of exams.

For an examination with very few applicants, you may be told to record your answers in the test booklet itself. Separate answer sheets are much more common. If this separate answer sheet is to be scored by machine – and this is often the case – it is highly important that you mark your answers correctly in order to get credit.

An electronic scoring machine is often used in civil service offices because of the speed with which papers can be scored. Machine-scored answer sheets must be marked with a pencil, which will be given to you. This pencil has a high graphite content which responds to the electronic scoring machine. As a matter of fact, stray dots may register as answers, so do not let your pencil rest on the answer sheet while you are pondering the correct answer. Also, if your pencil lead breaks or is otherwise defective, ask for another.

Since the answer sheet will be dropped in a slot in the scoring machine, be careful not to bend the corners or get the paper crumpled.

The answer sheet normally has five vertical columns of numbers, with 30 numbers to a column. These numbers correspond to the question numbers in your test booklet. After each number, going across the page are four or five pairs of dotted lines. These short dotted lines have small letters or numbers above them. The first two pairs may also have a "T" or "F" above the letters. This indicates that the first two pairs only are to be used if the questions are of the true-false type. If the questions are multiple choice, disregard the "T" and "F" and pay attention only to the small letters or numbers.

Answer your questions in the manner of the sample that follows:

32. The largest city in the United States is
    A. Washington, D.C.
    B. New York City
    C. Chicago
    D. Detroit
    E. San Francisco

1) Choose the answer you think is best. (New York City is the largest, so "B" is correct.)
2) Find the row of dotted lines numbered the same as the question you are answering. (Find row number 32)
3) Find the pair of dotted lines corresponding to the answer. (Find the pair of lines under the mark "B.")
4) Make a solid black mark between the dotted lines.

VI. BEFORE THE TEST

Common sense will help you find procedures to follow to get ready for an examination. Too many of us, however, overlook these sensible measures. Indeed, nervousness and fatigue have been found to be the most serious reasons why applicants fail to do their best on civil service tests. Here is a list of reminders:

- Begin your preparation early – Don't wait until the last minute to go scurrying around for books and materials or to find out what the position is all about.
- Prepare continuously – An hour a night for a week is better than an all-night cram session. This has been definitely established. What is more, a night a week for a month will return better dividends than crowding your study into a shorter period of time.
- Locate the place of the exam – You have been sent a notice telling you when and where to report for the examination. If the location is in a different town or otherwise unfamiliar to you, it would be well to inquire the best route and learn something about the building.
- Relax the night before the test – Allow your mind to rest. Do not study at all that night. Plan some mild recreation or diversion; then go to bed early and get a good night's sleep.
- Get up early enough to make a leisurely trip to the place for the test – This way unforeseen events, traffic snarls, unfamiliar buildings, etc. will not upset you.
- Dress comfortably – A written test is not a fashion show. You will be known by number and not by name, so wear something comfortable.

- Leave excess paraphernalia at home – Shopping bags and odd bundles will get in your way. You need bring only the items mentioned in the official notice you received; usually everything you need is provided. Do not bring reference books to the exam. They will only confuse those last minutes and be taken away from you when in the test room.
- Arrive somewhat ahead of time – If because of transportation schedules you must get there very early, bring a newspaper or magazine to take your mind off yourself while waiting.
- Locate the examination room – When you have found the proper room, you will be directed to the seat or part of the room where you will sit. Sometimes you are given a sheet of instructions to read while you are waiting. Do not fill out any forms until you are told to do so; just read them and be prepared.
- Relax and prepare to listen to the instructions
- If you have any physical problem that may keep you from doing your best, be sure to tell the test administrator. If you are sick or in poor health, you really cannot do your best on the exam. You can come back and take the test some other time.

VII. AT THE TEST

The day of the test is here and you have the test booklet in your hand. The temptation to get going is very strong. Caution! There is more to success than knowing the right answers. You must know how to identify your papers and understand variations in the type of short-answer question used in this particular examination. Follow these suggestions for maximum results from your efforts:

1) Cooperate with the monitor
The test administrator has a duty to create a situation in which you can be as much at ease as possible. He will give instructions, tell you when to begin, check to see that you are marking your answer sheet correctly, and so on. He is not there to guard you, although he will see that your competitors do not take unfair advantage. He wants to help you do your best.

2) Listen to all instructions
Don't jump the gun! Wait until you understand all directions. In most civil service tests you get more time than you need to answer the questions. So don't be in a hurry. Read each word of instructions until you clearly understand the meaning. Study the examples, listen to all announcements and follow directions. Ask questions if you do not understand what to do.

3) Identify your papers
Civil service exams are usually identified by number only. You will be assigned a number; you must not put your name on your test papers. Be sure to copy your number correctly. Since more than one exam may be given, copy your exact examination title.

4) Plan your time
Unless you are told that a test is a "speed" or "rate of work" test, speed itself is usually not important. Time enough to answer all the questions will be provided, but this does not mean that you have all day. An overall time limit has been set. Divide the total time (in minutes) by the number of questions to determine the approximate time you have for each question.

5) Do not linger over difficult questions

If you come across a difficult question, mark it with a paper clip (useful to have along) and come back to it when you have been through the booklet. One caution if you do this – be sure to skip a number on your answer sheet as well. Check often to be sure that you have not lost your place and that you are marking in the row numbered the same as the question you are answering.

6) Read the questions

Be sure you know what the question asks! Many capable people are unsuccessful because they failed to *read* the questions correctly.

7) Answer all questions

Unless you have been instructed that a penalty will be deducted for incorrect answers, it is better to guess than to omit a question.

8) Speed tests

It is often better NOT to guess on speed tests. It has been found that on timed tests people are tempted to spend the last few seconds before time is called in marking answers at random – without even reading them – in the hope of picking up a few extra points. To discourage this practice, the instructions may warn you that your score will be "corrected" for guessing. That is, a penalty will be applied. The incorrect answers will be deducted from the correct ones, or some other penalty formula will be used.

9) Review your answers

If you finish before time is called, go back to the questions you guessed or omitted to give them further thought. Review other answers if you have time.

10) Return your test materials

If you are ready to leave before others have finished or time is called, take ALL your materials to the monitor and leave quietly. Never take any test material with you. The monitor can discover whose papers are not complete, and taking a test booklet may be grounds for disqualification.

VIII. EXAMINATION TECHNIQUES

1) Read the general instructions carefully. These are usually printed on the first page of the exam booklet. As a rule, these instructions refer to the timing of the examination; the fact that you should not start work until the signal and must stop work at a signal, etc. If there are any *special* instructions, such as a choice of questions to be answered, make sure that you note this instruction carefully.

2) When you are ready to start work on the examination, that is as soon as the signal has been given, read the instructions to each question booklet, underline any key words or phrases, such as *least, best, outline, describe* and the like. In this way you will tend to answer as requested rather than discover on reviewing your paper that you *listed without describing*, that you selected the *worst* choice rather than the *best* choice, etc.

3) If the examination is of the objective or multiple-choice type – that is, each question will also give a series of possible answers: A, B, C or D, and you are called upon to select the best answer and write the letter next to that answer on your answer paper – it is advisable to start answering each question in turn. There may be anywhere from 50 to 100 such questions in the three or four hours allotted and you can see how much time would be taken if you read through all the questions before beginning to answer any. Furthermore, if you come across a question or group of questions which you know would be difficult to answer, it would undoubtedly affect your handling of all the other questions.

4) If the examination is of the essay type and contains but a few questions, it is a moot point as to whether you should read all the questions before starting to answer any one. Of course, if you are given a choice – say five out of seven and the like – then it is essential to read all the questions so you can eliminate the two that are most difficult. If, however, you are asked to answer all the questions, there may be danger in trying to answer the easiest one first because you may find that you will spend too much time on it. The best technique is to answer the first question, then proceed to the second, etc.

5) Time your answers. Before the exam begins, write down the time it started, then add the time allowed for the examination and write down the time it must be completed, then divide the time available somewhat as follows:
    - If 3-1/2 hours are allowed, that would be 210 minutes. If you have 80 objective-type questions, that would be an average of 2-1/2 minutes per question. Allow yourself no more than 2 minutes per question, or a total of 160 minutes, which will permit about 50 minutes to review.
    - If for the time allotment of 210 minutes there are 7 essay questions to answer, that would average about 30 minutes a question. Give yourself only 25 minutes per question so that you have about 35 minutes to review.

6) The most important instruction is to *read each question* and make sure you know what is wanted. The second most important instruction is to *time yourself properly* so that you answer every question. The third most important instruction is to *answer every question*. Guess if you have to but include something for each question. Remember that you will receive no credit for a blank and will probably receive some credit if you write something in answer to an essay question. If you guess a letter – say "B" for a multiple-choice question – you may have guessed right. If you leave a blank as an answer to a multiple-choice question, the examiners may respect your feelings but it will not add a point to your score. Some exams may penalize you for wrong answers, so in such cases *only*, you may not want to guess unless you have some basis for your answer.

7) Suggestions
    a. Objective-type questions
        1. Examine the question booklet for proper sequence of pages and questions
        2. Read all instructions carefully
        3. Skip any question which seems too difficult; return to it after all other questions have been answered
        4. Apportion your time properly; do not spend too much time on any single question or group of questions

5. Note and underline key words – *all, most, fewest, least, best, worst, same, opposite,* etc.
6. Pay particular attention to negatives
7. Note unusual option, e.g., unduly long, short, complex, different or similar in content to the body of the question
8. Observe the use of "hedging" words – *probably, may, most likely,* etc.
9. Make sure that your answer is put next to the same number as the question
10. Do not second-guess unless you have good reason to believe the second answer is definitely more correct
11. Cross out original answer if you decide another answer is more accurate; do not erase until you are ready to hand your paper in
12. Answer all questions; guess unless instructed otherwise
13. Leave time for review

 b. Essay questions
  1. Read each question carefully
  2. Determine exactly what is wanted. Underline key words or phrases.
  3. Decide on outline or paragraph answer
  4. Include many different points and elements unless asked to develop any one or two points or elements
  5. Show impartiality by giving pros and cons unless directed to select one side only
  6. Make and write down any assumptions you find necessary to answer the questions
  7. Watch your English, grammar, punctuation and choice of words
  8. Time your answers; don't crowd material

8) Answering the essay question

Most essay questions can be answered by framing the specific response around several key words or ideas. Here are a few such key words or ideas:

M's: manpower, materials, methods, money, management
P's: purpose, program, policy, plan, procedure, practice, problems, pitfalls, personnel, public relations

 a. Six basic steps in handling problems:
  1. Preliminary plan and background development
  2. Collect information, data and facts
  3. Analyze and interpret information, data and facts
  4. Analyze and develop solutions as well as make recommendations
  5. Prepare report and sell recommendations
  6. Install recommendations and follow up effectiveness

 b. Pitfalls to avoid
  1. *Taking things for granted* – A statement of the situation does not necessarily imply that each of the elements is necessarily true; for example, a complaint may be invalid and biased so that all that can be taken for granted is that a complaint has been registered

2. *Considering only one side of a situation* – Wherever possible, indicate several alternatives and then point out the reasons you selected the best one
3. *Failing to indicate follow up* – Whenever your answer indicates action on your part, make certain that you will take proper follow-up action to see how successful your recommendations, procedures or actions turn out to be
4. *Taking too long in answering any single question* – Remember to time your answers properly

IX. AFTER THE TEST

Scoring procedures differ in detail among civil service jurisdictions although the general principles are the same. Whether the papers are hand-scored or graded by machine we have described, they are nearly always graded by number. That is, the person who marks the paper knows only the number – never the name – of the applicant. Not until all the papers have been graded will they be matched with names. If other tests, such as training and experience or oral interview ratings have been given, scores will be combined. Different parts of the examination usually have different weights. For example, the written test might count 60 percent of the final grade, and a rating of training and experience 40 percent. In many jurisdictions, veterans will have a certain number of points added to their grades.

After the final grade has been determined, the names are placed in grade order and an eligible list is established. There are various methods for resolving ties between those who get the same final grade – probably the most common is to place first the name of the person whose application was received first. Job offers are made from the eligible list in the order the names appear on it. You will be notified of your grade and your rank as soon as all these computations have been made. This will be done as rapidly as possible.

People who are found to meet the requirements in the announcement are called "eligibles." Their names are put on a list of eligible candidates. An eligible's chances of getting a job depend on how high he stands on this list and how fast agencies are filling jobs from the list.

When a job is to be filled from a list of eligibles, the agency asks for the names of people on the list of eligibles for that job. When the civil service commission receives this request, it sends to the agency the names of the three people highest on this list. Or, if the job to be filled has specialized requirements, the office sends the agency the names of the top three persons who meet these requirements from the general list.

The appointing officer makes a choice from among the three people whose names were sent to him. If the selected person accepts the appointment, the names of the others are put back on the list to be considered for future openings.

That is the rule in hiring from all kinds of eligible lists, whether they are for typist, carpenter, chemist, or something else. For every vacancy, the appointing officer has his choice of any one of the top three eligibles on the list. This explains why the person whose name is on top of the list sometimes does not get an appointment when some of the persons lower on the list do. If the appointing officer chooses the second or third eligible, the No. 1 eligible does not get a job at once, but stays on the list until he is appointed or the list is terminated.

X. HOW TO PASS THE INTERVIEW TEST

The examination for which you applied requires an oral interview test. You have already taken the written test and you are now being called for the interview test – the final part of the formal examination.

You may think that it is not possible to prepare for an interview test and that there are no procedures to follow during an interview. Our purpose is to point out some things you can do in advance that will help you and some good rules to follow and pitfalls to avoid while you are being interviewed.

What is an interview supposed to test?

The written examination is designed to test the technical knowledge and competence of the candidate; the oral is designed to evaluate intangible qualities, not readily measured otherwise, and to establish a list showing the relative fitness of each candidate – as measured against his competitors – for the position sought. Scoring is not on the basis of "right" and "wrong," but on a sliding scale of values ranging from "not passable" to "outstanding." As a matter of fact, it is possible to achieve a relatively low score without a single "incorrect" answer because of evident weakness in the qualities being measured.

Occasionally, an examination may consist entirely of an oral test – either an individual or a group oral. In such cases, information is sought concerning the technical knowledges and abilities of the candidate, since there has been no written examination for this purpose. More commonly, however, an oral test is used to supplement a written examination.

Who conducts interviews?

The composition of oral boards varies among different jurisdictions. In nearly all, a representative of the personnel department serves as chairman. One of the members of the board may be a representative of the department in which the candidate would work. In some cases, "outside experts" are used, and, frequently, a businessman or some other representative of the general public is asked to serve. Labor and management or other special groups may be represented. The aim is to secure the services of experts in the appropriate field.

However the board is composed, it is a good idea (and not at all improper or unethical) to ascertain in advance of the interview who the members are and what groups they represent. When you are introduced to them, you will have some idea of their backgrounds and interests, and at least you will not stutter and stammer over their names.

What should be done before the interview?

While knowledge about the board members is useful and takes some of the surprise element out of the interview, there is other preparation which is more substantive. It *is* possible to prepare for an oral interview – in several ways:

1) Keep a copy of your application and review it carefully before the interview

This may be the only document before the oral board, and the starting point of the interview. Know what education and experience you have listed there, and the sequence and dates of all of it. Sometimes the board will ask you to review the highlights of your experience for them; you should not have to hem and haw doing it.

2) Study the class specification and the examination announcement

Usually, the oral board has one or both of these to guide them. The qualities, characteristics or knowledges required by the position sought are stated in these documents. They offer valuable clues as to the nature of the oral interview. For example, if the job involves supervisory responsibilities, the announcement will usually indicate that knowledge of modern supervisory methods and the qualifications of the candidate as a supervisor will be tested. If so, you can expect such questions, frequently in the form of a hypothetical situation which you are expected to solve. NEVER go into an oral without knowledge of the duties and responsibilities of the job you seek.

3) Think through each qualification required

Try to visualize the kind of questions you would ask if you were a board member. How well could you answer them? Try especially to appraise your own knowledge and background in each area, *measured against the job sought*, and identify any areas in which you are weak. Be critical and realistic – do not flatter yourself.

4) Do some general reading in areas in which you feel you may be weak

For example, if the job involves supervision and your past experience has NOT, some general reading in supervisory methods and practices, particularly in the field of human relations, might be useful. Do NOT study agency procedures or detailed manuals. The oral board will be testing your understanding and capacity, not your memory.

5) Get a good night's sleep and watch your general health and mental attitude

You will want a clear head at the interview. Take care of a cold or any other minor ailment, and of course, no hangovers.

What should be done on the day of the interview?

Now comes the day of the interview itself. Give yourself plenty of time to get there. Plan to arrive somewhat ahead of the scheduled time, particularly if your appointment is in the fore part of the day. If a previous candidate fails to appear, the board might be ready for you a bit early. By early afternoon an oral board is almost invariably behind schedule if there are many candidates, and you may have to wait. Take along a book or magazine to read, or your application to review, but leave any extraneous material in the waiting room when you go in for your interview. In any event, relax and compose yourself.

The matter of dress is important. The board is forming impressions about you – from your experience, your manners, your attitude, and your appearance. Give your personal appearance careful attention. Dress your best, but not your flashiest. Choose conservative, appropriate clothing, and be sure it is immaculate. This is a business interview, and your appearance should indicate that you regard it as such. Besides, being well groomed and properly dressed will help boost your confidence.

Sooner or later, someone will call your name and escort you into the interview room. *This is it.* From here on you are on your own. It is too late for any more preparation. But remember, you asked for this opportunity to prove your fitness, and you are here because your request was granted.

What happens when you go in?

The usual sequence of events will be as follows: The clerk (who is often the board stenographer) will introduce you to the chairman of the oral board, who will introduce you to the other members of the board. Acknowledge the introductions before you sit down. Do not be surprised if you find a microphone facing you or a stenotypist sitting by. Oral interviews are usually recorded in the event of an appeal or other review.

Usually the chairman of the board will open the interview by reviewing the highlights of your education and work experience from your application – primarily for the benefit of the other members of the board, as well as to get the material into the record. Do not interrupt or comment unless there is an error or significant misinterpretation; if that is the case, do not hesitate. But do not quibble about insignificant matters. Also, he will usually ask you some question about your education, experience or your present job – partly to get you to start talking and to establish the interviewing "rapport." He may start the actual questioning, or turn it over to one of the other members. Frequently, each member undertakes the questioning on a particular area, one in which he is perhaps most competent, so you can expect each member to participate in the examination. Because time is limited, you may also expect some rather abrupt switches in the direction the questioning takes, so do not be upset by it. Normally, a board member will not pursue a single line of questioning unless he discovers a particular strength or weakness.

After each member has participated, the chairman will usually ask whether any member has any further questions, then will ask you if you have anything you wish to add. Unless you are expecting this question, it may floor you. Worse, it may start you off on an extended, extemporaneous speech. The board is not usually seeking more information. The question is principally to offer you a last opportunity to present further qualifications or to indicate that you have nothing to add. So, if you feel that a significant qualification or characteristic has been overlooked, it is proper to point it out in a sentence or so. Do not compliment the board on the thoroughness of their examination – they have been sketchy, and you know it. If you wish, merely say, "No thank you, I have nothing further to add." This is a point where you can "talk yourself out" of a good impression or fail to present an important bit of information. Remember, *you close the interview yourself.*

The chairman will then say, "That is all, Mr. _____, thank you." Do not be startled; the interview is over, and quicker than you think. Thank him, gather your belongings and take your leave. Save your sigh of relief for the other side of the door.

How to put your best foot forward

Throughout this entire process, you may feel that the board individually and collectively is trying to pierce your defenses, seek out your hidden weaknesses and embarrass and confuse you. Actually, this is not true. They are obliged to make an appraisal of your qualifications for the job you are seeking, and they want to see you in your best light. Remember, they must interview all candidates and a non-cooperative candidate may become a failure in spite of their best efforts to bring out his qualifications. Here are 15 suggestions that will help you:

1) **Be natural – Keep your attitude confident, not cocky**

If you are not confident that you can do the job, do not expect the board to be. Do not apologize for your weaknesses, try to bring out your strong points. The board is interested in a positive, not negative, presentation. Cockiness will antagonize any board member and make him wonder if you are covering up a weakness by a false show of strength.

2) **Get comfortable, but don't lounge or sprawl**

Sit erectly but not stiffly. A careless posture may lead the board to conclude that you are careless in other things, or at least that you are not impressed by the importance of the occasion. Either conclusion is natural, even if incorrect. Do not fuss with your clothing, a pencil or an ashtray. Your hands may occasionally be useful to emphasize a point; do not let them become a point of distraction.

3) **Do not wisecrack or make small talk**

This is a serious situation, and your attitude should show that you consider it as such. Further, the time of the board is limited – they do not want to waste it, and neither should you.

4) Do not exaggerate your experience or abilities

In the first place, from information in the application or other interviews and sources, the board may know more about you than you think. Secondly, you probably will not get away with it. An experienced board is rather adept at spotting such a situation, so do not take the chance.

5) If you know a board member, do not make a point of it, yet do not hide it

Certainly you are not fooling him, and probably not the other members of the board. Do not try to take advantage of your acquaintanceship – it will probably do you little good.

6) Do not dominate the interview

Let the board do that. They will give you the clues – do not assume that you have to do all the talking. Realize that the board has a number of questions to ask you, and do not try to take up all the interview time by showing off your extensive knowledge of the answer to the first one.

7) Be attentive

You only have 20 minutes or so, and you should keep your attention at its sharpest throughout. When a member is addressing a problem or question to you, give him your undivided attention. Address your reply principally to him, but do not exclude the other board members.

8) Do not interrupt

A board member may be stating a problem for you to analyze. He will ask you a question when the time comes. Let him state the problem, and wait for the question.

9) Make sure you understand the question

Do not try to answer until you are sure what the question is. If it is not clear, restate it in your own words or ask the board member to clarify it for you. However, do not haggle about minor elements.

10) Reply promptly but not hastily

A common entry on oral board rating sheets is "candidate responded readily," or "candidate hesitated in replies." Respond as promptly and quickly as you can, but do not jump to a hasty, ill-considered answer.

11) Do not be peremptory in your answers

A brief answer is proper – but do not fire your answer back. That is a losing game from your point of view. The board member can probably ask questions much faster than you can answer them.

12) Do not try to create the answer you think the board member wants

He is interested in what kind of mind you have and how it works – not in playing games. Furthermore, he can usually spot this practice and will actually grade you down on it.

13) Do not switch sides in your reply merely to agree with a board member

Frequently, a member will take a contrary position merely to draw you out and to see if you are willing and able to defend your point of view. Do not start a debate, yet do not surrender a good position. If a position is worth taking, it is worth defending.

14) Do not be afraid to admit an error in judgment if you are shown to be wrong

The board knows that you are forced to reply without any opportunity for careful consideration. Your answer may be demonstrably wrong. If so, admit it and get on with the interview.

15) Do not dwell at length on your present job

The opening question may relate to your present assignment. Answer the question but do not go into an extended discussion. You are being examined for a *new* job, not your present one. As a matter of fact, try to phrase ALL your answers in terms of the job for which you are being examined.

Basis of Rating

Probably you will forget most of these "do's" and "don'ts" when you walk into the oral interview room. Even remembering them all will not ensure you a passing grade. Perhaps you did not have the qualifications in the first place. But remembering them will help you to put your best foot forward, without treading on the toes of the board members.

Rumor and popular opinion to the contrary notwithstanding, an oral board wants you to make the best appearance possible. They know you are under pressure – but they also want to see how you respond to it as a guide to what your reaction would be under the pressures of the job you seek. They will be influenced by the degree of poise you display, the personal traits you show and the manner in which you respond.

ABOUT THIS BOOK

This book contains tests divided into Examination Sections. Go through each test, answering every question in the margin. We have also attached a sample answer sheet at the back of the book that can be removed and used. At the end of each test look at the answer key and check your answers. On the ones you got wrong, look at the right answer choice and learn. Do not fill in the answers first. Do not memorize the questions and answers, but understand the answer and principles involved. On your test, the questions will likely be different from the samples. Questions are changed and new ones added. If you understand these past questions you should have success with any changes that arise. Tests may consist of several types of questions. We have additional books on each subject should more study be advisable or necessary for you. Finally, the more you study, the better prepared you will be. This book is intended to be the last thing you study before you walk into the examination room. Prior study of relevant texts is also recommended. NLC publishes some of these in our Fundamental Series. Knowledge and good sense are important factors in passing your exam. Good luck also helps. So now study this Passbook, absorb the material contained within and take that knowledge into the examination. Then do your best to pass that exam.

EXAMINATION SECTION

ARITHMETICAL REASONING

EXAMINATION SECTION
TEST 1

DIRECTIONS: Each question or incomplete statement is followed by several suggested answers or completions. Select the one that BEST answers the question or completes the statement. *PRINT THE LETTER OF THE CORRECT ANSWER IN THE SPACE AT THE RIGHT.*

1. A canvas tarpaulin measures 6 feet by 9 feet.
   The LARGEST circular area that can be covered completely by this tarpaulin is a circle with a diameter of _____ feet.

   A. 9 B. 8 C. 7 D. 6

2. The population of Maple Grove was 1,000 in 2006. In 2007, the population increased 40 percent, but in 2008, 2009, and 2010, the population decreased 20 percent, 10 percent, and 25 percent, respectively. (For each year, the percentage change in population is based upon a comparison with the preceding year.)
   At the end of this period, the population was MOST NEARLY

   A. 900 B. 850 C. 800 D. 750

3. The ratio of boys to girls in one school is 6 to 4. A second school contains half as many boys and twice as many girls as the first.
   The one of the following statements that is MOST accurate is that

   A. both schools have the same number of pupils
   B. the first school has 10 percent more pupils than the second
   C. the second school has 10 percent more pupils than the first
   D. there is not sufficient information to reach any conclusion about which school has more pupils

4. In a certain city, X number of cases of malaria have occurred over a 10-year period, resulting in Y number of deaths.
   The AVERAGE annual death rate from malaria in this city is

   A. Y/10 B. 10/X C. 10-X/Y D. $\frac{Y(10X)}{X+Y}$

5. A firemen's softball team wins 6 games out of the first 9 played. They go on to win all their remaining games and finish the season with a final average of games won of .750.
   The TOTAL number of games they played that season was

   A. 10 B. 12 C. 15 D. 18

6. While inspecting a cylindrical gravity tank for an automatic sprinkler system, a chief observes that the water in the tank is 10 feet deep and that the tank has a diameter of 9 feet. He asks the building manager how many gallons are in the tank and receives the reply, *About 10,000.* (Cubic foot of water contains 7 1/2 gallons.) Based on his own observation and calculations, the chief should

1._____

2._____

3._____

4._____

5._____

6._____

A. agree that the manager's answer is probably correct
B. disagree with the manager's answer; the answer is more nearly 20,000 gallons
C. disagree with the manager's answer; the answer is more nearly 15,000 gallons
D. disagree with the manager's answer; the answer is more nearly 5,000 gallons

7. The diagram at the right represents the storage space of a fire engine. The amount of space available for the storage of hose in the fire engine is MOST NEARLY _____ cubic feet.
   A. 40
   B. 75
   C. 540
   D. 600

7._____

8. If a piece of rope 100 feet long is cut so that one piece is 2/3 as long as the other piece, the length of the longer piece must be _____ feet.

   A. 60   B. 66 2/3   C. 70   D. 75

8._____

9. A water tank has a discharge valve which is capable of emptying the tank when full in two hours. It also has an inlet valve which can fill the tank, when empty, in four hours and a second inlet valve which can fill the tank, when empty, in six hours.
   If the tank is full and all three valves are opened fully, with water flowing through each valve to capacity, the tank will be emptied in _____ hours.

   A. 2
   B. 6
   C. 12
   D. a period of time which cannot be determined from the information given

9._____

10. Final grades in a history course are determined as follows:
    Class recitations - weight 50
    Weekly quizzes - weight 25
    Final examination - weight 25
    A student has an average of 60 on a class recitation and 80 on weekly quizzes.
    In order to receive a final grade of 75, he must obtain on his final examination a grade of

    A. 75   B. 80   C. 90   D. 100

10._____

11. Suppose that 8 inches of snow contribute as much water to the reservoir system as one inch of rain.
    If, during a snowstorm, an average of 12 inches of snow fell during a six-hour period, with drifts as high as three feet, the addition to the water supply as a result of this snowfall ultimately will be the equivalent of _____ inches of rain.

    A. 1 1/2
    B. 3
    C. 4 1/2
    D. an amount of rain which cannot be determined from the information given

11._____

12. A fire engine carries 900 feet of 2 1/2" hose, 500 feet of 2" hose, and 350 feet of 1 1/2" hose.
    Of the total hose carried, the percentage of 1 1/2" hose is MOST NEARLY

    A. 35   B. 30   C. 25   D. 20

    12.____

13. An engine company made 96 runs in the month of April, which was a decrease of 20% from the number of runs made in March.
    The number of runs made in March was MOST NEARLY

    A. 136   B. 128   C. 120   D. 110

    13.____

14. A water tank has a capacity of 6,000 gallons. Connected to the tank is a pump capable of supplying water at the rate of 25 gallons per minute, which goes into operation automatically when the water in the tank falls to the one-half mark.
    If we start with a full tank and drain the water from the tank at the rate of 50 gallons a minute, the tank can continue supplying water at the required rate for_____ hours.

    A. 2 1/2   B. 3   C. 3 1/2   D. 4

    14.____

15. Three firemen are assigned the task of cleaning fire apparatus which usually takes three men five hours to complete. After they have been working three hours, three additional firemen are assigned to help them. Assuming that they all work at the normal rate, the assignment of the additional men will reduce the time required to complete the task by _____ minutes.

    A. 20   B. 30   C. 50   D. 60

    15.____

16. Assume that at the beginning of the calendar year, an employee was earning $48,000 per year. On July 1st, he received an increase of $2,400 per year. On November 1st, he was promoted to a position paying $60,000 per year. The total earnings for the year were MOST NEARLY

    A. $51,000   B. $49,000   C. $50,000   D. $53,000

    16.____

17. Engine A leaves its firehouse at 1:48 P.M. and travels 3 miles to a fire at an average speed of 30 miles per hour. Engine B leaves its firehouse at 1:51 P.M. and travels 6 miles to the same fire at an average speed of 40 miles per hour.
    From the above facts, we may conclude that Engine A arrives _____ minutes _____ Engine B.

    A. 3; before   B. 6; before
    C. 3; after   D. 6; after

    17.____

18. A widely used formula for calculating the quantity of water discharged from a hose is $GPM = 29.7d^2/P$, where GPM = gallons per minute, d = diameter of the nozzle in inches, and P = pressure at the nozzle in pounds per square inch.
    If it takes 1 minute to extinguish a fire using a 1 1/2" nozzle at 100 pounds pressure per square inch, the number of gallons discharged is, according to the above formula, MOST NEARLY

    A. 730   B. 650   C. 690   D. 670

    18.____

19. The spring of a spring balance will stretch in proportion to the amount of weight placed on the balance.
    If a 2-pound weight placed on a certain balance stretches the spring 1/4", then a stretch in the spring of 1 3/4" will be caused by a weight of _____ lbs.

    A. 10   B. 12   C. 14   D. 16

20. In a yard 100 feet by 60 feet, a dog is tied by a leash to a stake driven into the ground in the center of the yard.
    If the dog is to be kept from going off the property, the MAXIMUM acceptable length of the leash is _____ feet.

    A. 60   B. 50   C. 30   D. 28

21. From a length of pipe 10 feet long, a 3 1/3 foot piece is to be cut.
    If the diameter of the 10-foot length is 5 inches, the diameter of the piece to be cut will be

    A. 5"   B. 2 1/3"   C. 2"   D. 1 2/3"

22. A certain crew consists of one foreman who is paid $15.00 per hour, 2 carpenters who are paid $12.60 per hour, 4 helpers who are paid $10.50 per hour, and 10 laborers who are paid $7.50 per hour.
    The average hourly earnings of the members of the crew is MOST NEARLY

    A. $11.40   B. $10.50   C. $10.05   D. $9.30

23. The fraction which is equivalent to the sum of .125, .25, .375, and .0625 is

    A. 5/8   B. 13/16   C. 7/8   D. 15/16

24. If the pay period of an employee is changed from every two weeks to twice a month, his gross pay (before deductions) from each pay period will

    A. increase by one-tenth
    B. increase by one-twelfth
    C. decrease by one-thirteenth
    D. decrease by one-fifteenth

25. In a certain state, the automobile license tags consist of two letters followed by three digits, e.g., AA-122. The MAXIMUM number of different combinations of numbers and letters which can be obtained under this system is MOST NEARLY

    A. 13,500   B. 75,000   C. 325,000   D. 675,000

KEY (CORRECT ANSWERS)

1.	D	11.	A
2.	D	12.	D
3.	C	13.	C
4.	A	14.	B
5.	B	15.	D
6.	D	16.	A
7.	C	17.	B
8.	A	18.	D
9.	C	19.	C
10.	D	20.	C

21. A
22. D
23. B
24. B
25. D

SOLUTIONS TO PROBLEMS

1. The largest circular area completely covered by the tarpaulin would have a diameter of the lesser of 6 ft. and 9 ft.

2. At the end of 2010, the population was $(1000)(1.40)(.80)(.90)(.75) = 756 \approx 750$.

3. Let 6x and 4x represent the number of boys and girls, respectively, at the first school. Then, 3x and 8x will represent the number of boys and girls, respectively, at the second school. The enrollment of the second school, 11x, is 10% higher than the enrollment at the first school, 10x.

4. Since Y deaths have occurred over a 10-year period due to malaria, the annual death rate caused by malaria is Y/10. X, the number of cases of malaria, has no effect on the annual death rate.

5. Let x = number of games played, after the first 9 games. Then, $(6+x)/(9+x) = .750$. Solving, x = 3. The total number of games played = 9 + 3 = 12.

6. Volume = $(\pi)(4.5)^2(10) \approx 636$ cu.ft. Then, $(636)(7\ 1/2) = 4770 \approx 5000$

7. 15x8x3 = 360; 15x6x2 = 180; 360 + 180 = 540 cu.ft.

8. Let 2x and 3x represent the two pieces. Then, 2x + 3x = 100. Solving, x = 20. The longer piece = (3)(20) = 60 ft.

9. Let x = number of hours required. Then, $\frac{x}{2} \cdot \frac{x}{4} \cdot \frac{x}{6} = 1$ Simplifying, x/12 = 1. Thus, x = 12

10. Let x = final exam grade. Then, $(60)(.50) + (80)(.25) + (x)(.25) = 75$. Simplifying, 50 + ,25x = 75. Solving, x = 100

11. If 8 in. of snow contribute 1 in. of rain, then 12 in. of snow contribute (1)(12/8) = 1 1/2 in. of rain.

12. 350 ÷ (900+500+350) = .20 = 20%

13. The number of runs in March was 96 ÷ .80 = 120

14. The time required to extract 3000 gallons at 50 gallons per minute = 3000 ÷ 50 = 60 min. = 1 hour. At this point, the tank is half full. Also, a pump begins replenishing the tank at 25 gallons per minute. Thus, the effect on draining has been slowed to 50 - 25 = 25 gallons per minute. To drain the remaining 3000 gallons will require 3000 ÷ 25 = 120 minutes = 2 hours. Total draining time = 3 hours.

15. (3)(5) = 15 man-hours. After 3 hours, 9 man-hours have been used. At this point, 6 men are working, and since only 6 man-hours remaining, the time needed is 1 hour = 60 minutes.

16. ($48,000)(1/2) + ($50,400)(1/3) + ($60,000)(1/6) = $50,800 ≈ $51,000

17. Engine A requires (3)(60/30) = 6 minutes to get to the fire.
    So, Engine A arrives at 1:54 PM. Engine B requires (6)(60/40) = 9 minutes to get to the fire. So, Engine B arrives at 2:00 PM. Thus, Engine A arrives 6 minutes before Engine B.

18. GPM = $(29.7)(1.5)^2(\sqrt{100})$ = 668.25 ≈ 670

19. Let x = required number of pounds. Then, 2/x = 1/4/1 3/4.
    So, 1/4x = 3 1/2. Solving, x = 14

20. The shorter of the two dimensions is 60 ft. If the dog is in the center of the yard, the maximum length allowed for the leash is 60/2 = 30 ft.

21. The diameter of the cut piece = diameter of entire pipe = 5"

22. [($15.00)(1)+($12.60)(2)+($10.50)(4)+($7.50)(10)]/17 = $157.20/17 9.25 (closest answer in answer key is $9.30).

23. .125 + .25 + .375 + .0625 = .8125 = 13/16

24. Let x = annual pay. Then, x/26 = pay every two weeks, whereas pay every half month. His increase is $\frac{x}{24} - \frac{x}{26} = \frac{x}{312}$, which represents a fractional increase of $\frac{x}{312} / \frac{x}{26} = \frac{1}{12}$

25. The number of different license tags = (26)(26)(10)(10)(10) = 676,000 (closest answer in answer key is 675,000).

TEST 2

DIRECTIONS: Each question or incomplete statement is followed by several suggested answers or completions. Select the one that BEST answers the question or completes the statement. *PRINT THE LETTER OF THE CORRECT ANSWER IN THE SPACE AT THE RIGHT.*

1. If cast iron weighs 450 pounds per cubic foot, the weight of a solid cast iron manhole cover 2 feet in diameter and 1 inch thick is MOST NEARLY _____ pounds.   1._____
    A. 94 B. 118 C. 136 D. 164

2. The sum of 2 5/8, 3 3/16, 1 1/2, and 4 1/4 is   2._____
    A. 9 13/16 B. 10 7/16 C. 11 9/16 D. 13 3/16

3. A pump is able to fill a tank holding 15,000 gallons in 2 hours and 30 minutes. Pumping at the same rate, an empty 60,000 gallon tank can be filled in   3._____
    A. 10 hours B. 10 hours, 30 minutes
    C. 11 hours D. 11 hours, 30 minutes

4. Assume you want to add 10,000 gallons of water to a tank. If you pump water into the tank at the rate of 100 gallons per minute for one hour and 50 gallons per minute after the first hour, the total time required to add the 10,000 gallons is MOST NEARLY   4._____
    A. 1 hour, 20 minutes B. 2 hours
    C. 2 hours, 20 minutes D. 3 hours

5. A tank 25 feet long, 15 feet wide, and 10 feet deep is enlarged by extending the length another 25 feet.
    The enlarged tank will be able to hold _____ more than the original tank.   5._____
    A. 50% B. 100% C. 150% D. 200%

6. If cast iron weighs 450 pounds per cubic foot, the weight of a solid cast iron manhole cover 4 feet in diameter and 1 inch thick is MOST NEARLY _____ pounds.   6._____
    A. 188 B. 236 C. 328 D. 471

7. If four men work seven hours during the day, the number of man-hours of work done is   7._____
    A. 4 B. 7 C. 11 D. 28

8. If it takes four men fourteen days to do a certain job, seven men working at the same rate should be able to do the same job in _____ days.   8._____
    A. 8 B. 7 C. 6 D. 5

9. A truck leaves the garage at 9:26 A.M. and returns the same day at 3:43 P.M. The period of time that the truck was away from the garage is MOST NEARLY _____ hours, _____ minutes.   9._____
    A. 5; 17 B. 5; 43 C. 6; 17 D. 6; 26

10. Assume that it takes 6 men 8 days to do a certain job. Working at the same speed, the number of days that it will take 4 men to do this job is

   A. 9   B. 10   C. 12   D. 14

11. The sum of 3 5/8 + 4 1/4 + 6 1/2 + 7 1/8 is

   A. 20 7/8   B. 21 1/4   C. 21 1/2   D. 22 1/8

12. The fraction which is equal to .0625 is

   A. 1/64   B. 3/64   C. 1/16   D. 5/8

13. The volume, in cubic feet, of a rectangular coal bin 8 feet long by 5 feet wide by 7 feet high is MOST NEARLY

   A. 40   B. 56   C. 186   D. 280

14. Assume that a car travels at a constant speed of 36 miles per hour.
    The speed of this car, in feet per second, is MOST NEARLY (one mile equals 5,280 ft.)

   A. 3   B. 24.6   C. 52.8   D. 879.8

15. If one-third of a 19-foot length of lumber is cut off, the length of the remaining piece will measure APPROXIMATELY

   A. 8'8"   B. 9'8"   C. 12'8"   D. 13'8"

16. The circumference of a circle having a diameter of 10" is MOST NEARLY _____ inches.

   A. 3.14   B. 18.72   C. 24.96   D. 31.4

17. Assume that in the purchase of paint, the seller quotes a discount of 10%.
    If the price per gallon is $19.05, the actual payment, in dollars per gallon, is MOST NEARLY

   A. $17.15   B. $17.85   C. $18.75   D. $19.50

18. Assume that a cubic foot of water contains 7 1/2 gallons. The number of gallons of water which could be contained in a rectangular tank 3 feet long, 2 feet wide, and 2 feet deep is MOST NEARLY

   A. 12   B. 45   C. 90   D. 120

19. The volume, in cubic feet, of a slab of concrete that is 5'0" wide, 6'0" long, and 0'6" in depth is MOST NEARLY

   A. 15.0   B. 13.5   C. 12.0   D. 10.5

20. The sum of the following pipe lengths, 22 1/8", 7 3/4", 19 7/16", and 43 5/8", is

   A. 91 7/8"   B. 92 1/16"   C. 92 1/2"   D. 92 15/16"

21. The area, in square feet, of a plant floor that is 42 feet wide and 75 feet long is

   A. 3,150   B. 3,100   C. 3.075   D. 2,760

22. The sum of the following dimensions, 1 5/8, 2 1/4, 4 1/16, and 3 3/16, is

   A. 10 15/16   B. 11   C. 11 1/8   D. 11 1/4

23. Assume that six men, working together at the same rate of speed, can complete a certain job in 3 hours.
If, however, there were only four men available to do this job, and they all worked at the same rate of speed, to complete this job would take MOST NEARLY _____ hours.

    A. 4 1/4   B. 4 1/2   C. 4 3/4   D. 5

23.____

24. Due to unforeseen difficulties, a job which would normally take 17 hours to complete was actually completed in 21 hours.
This represents a percent increase over the normal time of MOST NEARLY

    A. 19%   B. 2.4%   C. 24%   D. 124%

24.____

25. Truck A costs $30,000 and gets 12 mpg and truck B costs $35,000 and gets 15 mpg. After 1 year driving 12,000 miles, how much would be saved by purchasing truck A if gasoline costs $1.50 per gallon?

    A. $1,000   B. $3,000   C. $4,700   D. $6,000

25.____

KEY (CORRECT ANSWERS)

1. B		11. C	
2. C		12. C	
3. A		13. D	
4. C		14. C	
5. B		15. C	
6. D		16. D	
7. D		17. A	
8. A		18. C	
9. C		19. A	
10. C		20. D	

    21. A
    22. C
    23. B
    24. C
    25. C

SOLUTIONS TO PROBLEMS

1. $(450)(\pi)(1)^2(1/12) \approx 118$ pounds. (Note: $V = \pi R^2 H$)

2. 2 5/8 + 3 3/16 + 1 1/2 + 4 1/4 = 10 25/16 = 11 9/16

3. To fill a 60,000 gallon tank would require (4)(2 1/2 hrs.) = 10 hrs.

4. After 1 hour, (100)(60) = 6000 gallons have been added. To add the remaining 4000 gallons will require 4000 ÷ 50 = 80 minutes = 1 hour 20 minutes. Thus, total time needed is 2 hrs. 20 min.

5. The original volume = (25)(15)(10) = 3750 cu.ft., and the new volume = (50)(15)(10) = 7500 cu.ft. The increased volume of 3750 represents an increase of (3750/3750)(100) = 100%.

6. $(450)(\pi)(2)^2(1/12) \approx 471$ pounds

7. (4)(7) = 28 man-hours

8. (4)(14) = 56 man-days. Then, 56 ÷ 7 = 8 days

9. From 9:26 A.M. to 3:43 P.M. = 6 hrs. 17 min.

10. (6)(8) = 48 man-days. Then, 48 ÷ 4 = 12 days

11. 3 5/8 + 4 1/4 + 6 1/2 + 7 1/8 = 20 12/8 = 21 1/2

12. .0625 = 625/10,000 = 1/16

13. (8)(5)(7) = 280 cu.ft.

14. (36)(5280) = 190,080 ft. per hour. Since there are 3600 seconds in 1 hour, the speed = 190,080 ÷ 3600 = 52.8 ft. per second.

15. 19' - 1/3(19') = 12 2/3, = 12'8"

16. Circumference = $(\pi)(10")$ 31.4"

17. ($19.05)(.90) ≈ $17.15

18. (7 1/2)(3)(2)(2) = 90 gallons

19. (5)(6)(1/2) = 15 cu.ft.

20. 22 1/8" + 7 3/4" + 19 7/16" + 43 5/8" = 91 31/16" = 92 15/16"

21. Area = (42)(75) = 3150 sq.ft.

22. 1 5/8 + 2 1/4 + 4 1/16 + 3 3/16 = 10 18/16 = 11 1/8

23. (6) (3) = 18 man-hours. Then, 18 / 4 = 4 1/2 hours

24. 21 - 17 = 4. Then, 4/17 ≈ 24%

25. For Truck A, the expenses are $30,000 + (1000)($1.50) = $31,500 For Truck B, the expenses are $35,000 + (800)($1.50) = $36,200. $36,200 - $31,500 = $4,700

TEST 3

DIRECTIONS: Each question or incomplete statement is followed by several suggested answers or completions. Select the one that BEST answers the question or completes the statement. *PRINT THE LETTER OF THE CORRECT ANSWER IN THE SPACE AT THE RIGHT.*

1. Assume that a light maintainer and his helper replaced 25 lamps on one round of their assigned territory.
   If it took two hours to complete this round, and the maintainer's pay rate was $9.60 per hour and the helper's rate was $8.40 per hour, the labor cost of replacing each burned out lamp averaged _____ cents.
   A. 18   B. 36   C. 72   D. 144

   1._____

2. A certain power distribution job will require two main-tainers at $16.00 per hour and two helpers at $13.20 per hour. The job will take three 8-hour days to complete and will require 6 hours of planning and supervision by a foreman at $19.60 per hour.
   The TOTAL labor cost for this job is
   A. $264.80   B. $501.60   C. $818.40   D. $1,519.20

   2._____

3. Two identical containers are partly filled with bolts and weigh 40 lbs. and 75 lbs., respectively. To save storage space, all the bolts are put in one of the containers. The two containers now weigh 5 lbs. and 110 lbs., respectively.
   If three bolts weigh 1/2 lb., the TOTAL number of bolts is
   A. 210   B. 450   C. 630   D. 660

   3._____

4. The sum of the following dimensions, 2'7 1/2", 1'8 1/2", 2'1/16", and 3/4", is
   A. 5'15 9/16"   B. 5'15 11/16"
   C. 5'7/16"   D. 6'4 9/16"

   4._____

5. If a 3-foot length of contact rail weighs 150 pounds, then 39 feet of contact rail weighs _____ pounds.
   A. 1,850   B. 1,900   C. 1,950   D. 2,000

   5._____

6. The sum of the following dimensions, 3'2 1/2", 8 7/8", 2'6 3/8", 2'9 3/4", and 1'0", is
   A. 9'3 1/4"   B. 10'3 1/4"   C. 10'7 1/4"   D. 16'7 1/4"

   6._____

7. If a drawing for a contact rail installation is made to a scale of 1 1/2" to the foot, the drawing is said to be one _____ size.
   A. sixteenth   B. eight   C. quarter   D. half

   7._____

8. If a drawing has a scale of 1/4" = 1', a dimension of 1 3/4" on the drawing would be equal to
   A. 4'   B. 5'   C. 6'   D. 7'

   8._____

9. A reel weighs 600 lbs. when fully loaded with cable and 200 lbs. when empty.
   If the cable weighs 2.5 lbs. per foot, the number of reels a foreman should order for a job requiring 700 feet of this cable is _____ reels.
   A. 2   B. 3   C. 4   D. 5

   9._____

10. If the scale on a working drawing is shown as 1/4" = 1', a scaled measurement of 4 1/2 inches represents an actual length of _____ feet.

    A. 8   B. 9   C. 16   D. 18

11. A gap on the third rail starts at a subway column marked 217+79. The gap extends 68 feet to another column marked 217+11.
    A column midway between these columns would be marked 217+_____

    A. 34   B. 39   C. 45   D. 68

12. Assume a foreman decided that 100 contact rail ties need replacing. Each tie measures 9' x 6" x 8".
    In providing room for storing these ties at the job site, the MINIMUM storage volume required is APPROXIMATELY _____ cubic feet.

    A. 300   B. 360   C. 432   D. 576

13. Assume a certain job was done a year ago and took 8 men a total of 5 days to complete. The records show that each day involved 5 hours of overtime for half the men. Your assistant supervisor now assigns you the identical job to be done using 6 men and no overtime.
    The MINIMUM number of regular work days that should be scheduled for this job is _____ days.

    A. 13   B. 11   C. 9   D. 6

14. The sum of the following dimensions, 12'11 3/16", 9'8 5/8", 7'3 3/4", 5'2 1/2", and 3'1 1/4", is

    A. 39'5 9/16"   B. 38'3 5/16"
    C. 36'2 3/8"   D. 35'1 7/8"

15. If the scale on a drawing is 1/4" to the foot, then a 5/8" measurement would represent an actual length of

    A. 5'4"   B. 4'8"   C. 2'6"   D. 1'3"

16. The sum of 1 9/16", 3 1/2", 7 3/8", 10 3/4", and 12 5/8" is

    A. 33 11/16"   B. 34 13/16"   C. 35 11/16"   D. 35 13/16"

17. A reel containing an unknown length of cable weighs 340 pounds.
    If the empty reel weighs 119 lbs. and the cable weighs 0.85 lb. per foot, the number of feet of cable on the reel is

    A. 140   B. 260   C. 400   D. 540

18. If the scale on a shop drawing is 1/4" to the foot, then a part which measures 3 3/8 inches long on the drawing has an actual length of_____ feet _____ inches.

    A. 12; 6   B. 13; 6   C. 13; 9   D. 14; 9

19. Taking into account time and one-half payment for time over 40 hours of work, the gross pay of an employee who works 43 hours in a week at a rate of pay of $5.34 per hour is

    A. $213.60   B. $229.62   C. $237.63   D. $245.64

20. The sum of 0.365 + 3.941 + 10.676 + 0.784 is

   A. 13.766   B. 15.666   C. 15.756   D. 15.766

21. An air conditioning unit is rated at 1000 watts. The unit is run for 10 hours per day, five days per week. If the cost for electrical energy is 50 cents per kilowatt-hour, the weekly cost for electricity should be

   A. $2.50   B. $5.00   C. $25.00   D. $250.00

22. Assume that the cost of a certain wiring installation is broken down as follows: Materials $1,200, Labor $800, and Rental of equipment $400.
   The percentage of the total cost of the job that can be charged to Labor is MOST NEARLY

   A. 12.3   B. 33.3   C. 40.0   D. 66.6

23. Assume that it takes 4 electrician's helpers 6 days to do a certain job.
   Working at the same rate of speed, the number of days it will take 3 electrician's helpers to do the same job is

   A. 6   B. 7   C. 8   D. 9

24. Assume that a 120-volt, 25-cycle magnetic coil is to be rewound to operate properly on 60-cycles at the same voltage.
   If the coil at 25-cycles has 1,000 turns, at 60-cycles the number of turns should be MOST NEARLY

   A. 2,400   B. 1,200   C. 416   D. 208

25. A light maintainer whose rate is $14.40 per hour is assigned to replace burned-out station and tunnel lamps. During 4 hours, he replaces 28 lamps.
   The average labor cost for replacing each of these burned-out lamps was NEAREST to

   A. 56¢   B. $1.04   C. $2.00   D. $3.60

KEY (CORRECT ANSWERS)

1.	D	11.	C
2.	D	12.	A
3.	C	13.	C
4.	D	14.	B
5.	C	15.	C
6.	B	16.	D
7.	B	17.	B
8.	D	18.	B
9.	D	19.	C
10.	D	20.	D

21. C
22. B
23. C
24. C
25. C

SOLUTIONS TO PROBLEMS

1. (2)($9.60+$8.40) = $36.00. Then, $36.00 ÷ 25 = $1.44 or 144 cents.

2. (2)($16.00)(24) + (2)($13.20)(24) + (6)($19.60) = $1519.20

3. An empty container weighs 5 lbs., so the container which contains bolts and weighs 110 lbs. actually has 105 lbs. of bolts. Since 3 bolts weigh 1/2 lb., 105 lbs. would contain (105/1/2)(3) = 630 bolts.

4. 2'7 1/4" + 1'8 1/2" + 2'1/16" + 3/4" = 5'15 25/16" = 6 '4 9/16"

5. 39 feet of rail weighs (13)(150) = 1950 pounds

6. 3'2 1/4" + 8 7/8" + 2'6 3/8" + 2'9 3/4" + 1'0" = 8'25 18/8" = 10'3 1/4"

7. 1 1/2"/1" = 3/2.1/12=1/8

8. l 3/4" ÷ 1/4" = 7 Then, (7)(1') = 7'

9. 600 - 200 = 400. Then, 400 ÷ 2.5 = 160 ft. of cable per reel. Since 700 ft. of cable is needed, 700/160 = 4.375, which means 5 reels will be required (must round up).

10. 4 1/2" ÷ 1/4" = 9/2 4/1 = 18 Then, (18)(1') = 18'

11. Half of 68 = 34; 11 + 34 = 45; 79 - 34 = 45

12. (100)(9')(1/2')(2/3') = 300 cu.ft.

13. Number of man-days = (4)(5) + (4)(5)(1 5/8) =52.5
    For 6 men working only 8-hour days, 52.5 ÷ 6 = 8.75 = 9 days needed.

14. 12'11 3/16" + 9'8 5/8" + 7'3 3/4" + 5'2 1/2" + 3'1 1/4" = 36'25 37/16" = 38'3 5/16"

15. 5/8" ÷ 1/4" = 5/8 . 4/1 = 2 1/2. Then, (2 1/2)(1') = 2'6"

16. 1 9/16" + 3 1/2" + 7 3/8" + 10 3/4" + 12 5/8" = 33 45/16" = 35 13/36"

17. 340 - 119 = 221 lbs. Then, 221 ÷ .85 = 260 ft.

18. 3 3/8" ÷ 1/4" = 27/8 . 4/1 = 13/ 1/2. Then, (13 1/2) (1') = 13 ft. 6 in.

19. (40)($5.34) + (3)($5.34)(1.5) = $237.63

20. 0.365 +3.941 + 10.676 + 0.784 = 15.766

21. (1000)(10)(5) = 50,000 watt-hours = 50 kilowatt-hours. Then, (50)($.50) = $25.00

22. $800 / ($1200+$800+$400) = 1/3 ≈ 33.3%

23. (4)(6) = 24. Then, 24/3 = 8 days

24. Let x = number of required turns. Since the number of cycles varies inversely as the number of turns, 25/60 = x/1000.
    Solving, x 416 (actually 416 2/3)

25. ($14.40)(4) = $57.60. Then, $57.60 ÷ 28 ≈ $2.06

ARITHMETICAL REASONING
EXAMINATION SECTION
TEST 1

DIRECTIONS: Each question or incomplete statement is followed by several suggested answers or completions. Select the one that BEST answers the question or completes the statement. *PRINT THE LETTER OF THE CORRECT ANSWER IN THE SPACE AT THE RIGHT.*

1.

   In the above sketch of a 3" pipeline, the distance X is MOST NEARLY _____ inches.

   A. 3 1/8   B. 3 1/2   C. 3 1/2   D. 3 5/8

2. The fraction 9/64 is MOST NEARLY equal to

   A. .1375   B. .1406   C. .1462   D. .1489

3. The sum of the following dimensions 1'2 3/16", 1'5 1/2", and 1'4 5/8" is

   A. 3'11 15/16"   B. 4' 5/16"
   C. 4'11/16"   D. 4'1 5/8"

4. The scale on a plumbing drawing is 1/8" = 1 foot.
   A horizontal line measuring 3 5/16" on the drawing would represent a length of _____ feet.

   A. 24.9   B. 26.5   C. 28.3   D. 30.2

5. Assume that a water meter reads 50,631 cubic feet and the previous reading was 39,842 cubic feet.
   If the charge for water is 23¢ per 100 cubic feet or any fraction thereof, the bill for the amount of water used since the previous meter reading will be

   A. $24.22   B. $24.38   C. $24.84   D. $24.95

6. At a certain premises, the water consumption was 4 percent higher in 2015 than it was in 2014.
   If the water consumption for 2015 was 9,740 cubic feet, then the water consumption for 2014 was MOST NEARLY _____ cubic feet.

   A. 9,320   B. 9,350   C. 9,365   D. 9,390

7. A pump delivers water at a constant rate of 40 gallons per minute.
   If there are 7.5 gallons to a cubic foot of water, the time it will take to fill a tank 6 feet x 5 feet x 4 feet is MOST NEARLY _____ minutes.

   A. 15   B. 22.5   C. 28.5   D. 30

8. The total weight, in pounds, of three lengths of 3" cast-iron pipe 7'6" long, weighing 14.5 pounds per foot, and four lengths of 4" cast-iron pipe each 5'0" long, weighing 13.0 pounds per foot, is MOST NEARLY

   A. 540   B. 585   C. 600   D. 665

9. The water pressure at the bottom of a column of water 34 feet high is 14.7 lbs./sq.in. The water pressure in lbs./sq.in. at the bottom of the column of water 12 feet high is MOST NEARLY

   A. 3   B. 5   C. 7   D. 9

10. The number of cubic yards of earth that would be removed when digging a trench 8 feet wide x 9 feet deep x 63 feet long is

    A. 56   B. 168   C. 314   D. 504

11. On test, a meter registered one cubic foot for each 1 1/3 cubic feet of water that passed through it.
    If the meter had a reading of 1,200 cubic feet, we may conclude that the CORRECT amount should be _____ cubic feet.

    A. 800   B. 900   C. 1,500   D. 1,600

12. A water use meter reads 87,463 cubic feet.
    If the previous reading was 17,377 cubic feet and the rate charged is 15 cents per 100 cubic feet, the bill for water use during this period is about

    A. $45.00   B. $65.00   C. $85.00   D. $105.00

13. Under proper conditions, the one of the following groups of pipes that gives the same flow in gals/min as one 6" diameter pipe is (neglect friction) _____ pipes of _____ diameter each.

    A. 3; 3"   B. 4; 3"   C. 2; 4"   D. 3; 4"

14. A roof tank is used to furnish the domestic water supply to a ten story building. This tank has a capacity of 5,900 gallons. At 10:00 A.M. one morning, the tank is half full.
    If water is being used at the rate of 50 gals/min, the pump which is used to fill the tank has a rated capacity of 90 gals/min, the time it would take to fill the tank under these conditions is MOST NEARLY _____ hour(s), _____ minutes.

    A. 2; 8   B. 1; 14   C. 2; 32   D. 1; 2

15. The number of gallons of water contained in a cylindrical swimming pool 8 feet in diameter and filled to a depth of 3 feet 6 inches is MOST NEARLY (assume 7.5 gallons = 1 cubic foot)

    A. 30   B. 225   C. 1,320   D. 3,000

16. The charge for metered water is 52 1/2 cents per hundred cubic feet, with a minimum charge of $21 per annum. Of the following, the SMALLEST water usage in hundred cubic feet that would result in a charge GREATER than the minimum is

    A. 39   B. 40   C. 41   D. 42

17. The annual frontage rent on a one-story building 40 ft. in length is $735.00. For each additional story, $52.50 per annum is added to the frontage rent. For demolition, the charge for wetting down is 3/8 of the annual frontage charge.
    The charge for wetting down a building six stories in height, with a 40 ft. frontage, is MOST NEARLY

    A. $369   B. $371   C. $372   D. $374

18. If the drawing of a piping layout is made to a scale of 1/4" equals one foot, then a 7'9" length of piping would be represented by a scaled length on the drawing of APPROXIMATELY _____ inches.

    A. 2   B. 7 3/4   C. 23 1/4   D. 31

19. A plumbing sketch is drawn to a scale of eighth-size. A line measuring 3" on the sketch would be equivalent to _____ feet.

    A. 2   B. 6   C. 12   D. 24

20. If 500 feet of pipe weighs 800 lbs., the number of pounds that 120 feet will weigh is MOST NEARLY

    A. 190   B. 210   C. 230   D. 240

21. If a trench is excavated 3'0" wide by 5'6" deep and 50 feet long, the total number of cubic yards of earth removed is MOST NEARLY

    A. 30   B. 90   C. 150   D. 825

22. Assume that a plumber earns $86,500 per year.
    If eighteen percent of his pay is deducted for taxes and social security, his net weekly pay will be APPROXIMATELY

    A. $1,326   B. $1,365   C. $1,436   D. $1,457.50

23. Assume that a plumbing installation is made up of the following fixtures and groups of fixtures: 12 bathroom groups each containing one W.C., one lavatory, and one bathtub with shower; 12 bathroom groups each containing one W.C., one lavatory, one bathtub, and one shower stall; 24 combination kitchen fixtures; 4 floor drains; 6 slop sinks without flushing rim; and 2 shower stalls (or shower bath).
    The total number of fixtures for the above plumbing installation is MOST NEARLY

    A. 60   B. 95   C. 120   D. 210

24. A triangular opening in a wall forms a 30-60 degree right triangle.
    If the longest side measures 12'0", then the shortest side will measure

    A. 3'0"   B. 4'0"   C. 6'0"   D. 8'0"

4 (#1)

25. You are directed to cut 4 pieces of pipe, one each of the following length: 2'6 1/4", 3'9 3/8", 4'7 5/8", and 5'8 7/8".
The total length of these 4 pieces is

 A. 15'7 1/4" B. 15'9 3/8" C. 16'5 7/8" D. 16'8 1/8"

25.___

KEY (CORRECT ANSWERS)

1.	A	11.	D
2.	B	12.	D
3.	B	13.	B
4.	B	14.	B
5.	C	15.	C
6.	C	16.	C
7.	B	17.	D
8.	B	18.	A
9.	B	19.	A
10.	B	20.	A

21. A
22. B
23. C
24. C
25. D

SOLUTIONS TO PROBLEMS

1. 8'3 1/2" + x + x = 8'9 3/4" Then, 2x = 6 1/4", so x = 3 1/8"

2. 9/64 = .140625 = .1406

3. 1'2 3/16" + 1'5 1/2" +1'4 5/8" = 3'11 21/16" = 4'5/16"

4. 3 5/16" ÷ 1/8" =53/16 x 8/1 = 26.5. Then, (26.5)(1 ft.) = 26.5 feet

5. 50,631 - 39,842 = 10,789; 10,789 ÷ 100 = 107.89
    Since the cost is .23 per 100 cubic feet or any fraction thereof, the cost will be
    (.23)(107) + .23 = $24.84

6. 9740 ÷ 1.04 = 9365 cu.ft.

7. 40 ÷ 7.5 = 5 1/3 cu.ft. of water per minute. The volume = (6)(5)(4) = 120 cu.ft. Thus, the number of minutes needed to fill the tank is 120 ÷ 5 1/3 = 22.5

8. 3" pipe: 3 x 7'6" = 22 1/2' x 14.5 lbs. = 326.25
    4" pipe: 4 x 5' = 20' x 13 lbs. = 260
    326.25 + 260 = 586.25 (most nearly 585)

9. Let x = pressure. Then, 34/12 = 14.7/x. So, 34x = 176.4
    Solving, x ≈ 5 lbs./sq.in.

10. (8)(9)(63) = 4536 cu.ft. Since 1 cu.yd. = 27 cu.ft., 4536 cu.ft. is equivalent to 168 cu.yds.

11. Let x = correct amount. Then, $\dfrac{1}{1200} = \dfrac{1\frac{1}{3}}{x}$. Solving, x = 1600

12. 87,463 - 17,377 = 70,086; and 70,086 ÷ 100 = 700.86 ≈ 700 Then, (700)(.15) = $105.00

13. Cross-sectional area of a 6" diameter pipe = $(\pi)(3")^2 = 9\pi$ sq. in. Note that the combined cross-sectional areas of four 3" diameter pipes = $(4)(\pi)(1.5")^2 = 9\pi$ sq. in.

14. 90 - 50 = 40 gals/min. Then, 2950 ÷ 40 = 73.75 min. ≈ 1 hr. 14 min.

15. Volume = $(\pi)(4)^2(3\ 1/2) = 56\pi$ cu.ft. Then, $(56\pi)(7.5) = 1320$ gals.

16. For 4100 cu.ft., the charge of (.525)(41) = $21,525 > $21

17. Rent = $73,500 + (5)($52.50) = $997,50. For demolition, the charge = (3/8)($997.50) $374

18. (1/4")(7.75) = 2"

19. (3")(8) = 24" = 2 ft.

6 (#1)

20. Let x = weight. Then, 500/800 = 120/x . Solving, x = 192 190 lbs.

21. (3')(5 1/2')(50') = 825 cu.ft. Then, 825 ÷ 27 ≈ 30 cu.yds.

22. Net pay = (.82)($86,500) = $70,930/yr. Weekly pay = $70,930 ÷ 52 ≈ $1365

23. (12x3) + (12x4) +24+4+6+2= 120

24. The shortest side = (1/2)(hypotenuse) = (1/2)(12') = 6'

25. 2'6 1/4" + 3'9 3/8" + 4'7 5/8" + 5'8 7/8 " = 14'30 17/8" = 16'8 1/8"

TEST 2

DIRECTIONS: Each question or incomplete statement is followed by several suggested answers or completions. Select the one that BEST answers the question or completes the statement. *PRINT THE LETTER OF THE CORRECT ANSWER IN THE SPACE AT THE RIGHT.*

1. The sum of the following pipe lengths, 15 5/8", 8 3/4", 30 5/16" and 20 1/2", is   1._____

   A. 77 1/8"   B. 76 3/16"   C. 75 3/16"   D. 74 5/16"

2. If the outside diameter of a pipe is 6 inches and the wall thickness is 1/2 inch, the inside area of this pipe, in square inches, is MOST NEARLY   2._____

   A. 15.7   B. 17.3   C. 19.6   D. 23.8

3. Three lengths of pipe 1'10", 3'2 1/2", and 5'7 1/2", respectively, are to be cut from a pipe 14'0" long.
   Allowing 1/8" for each pipe cut, the length of pipe remaining is   3._____

   A. 3'1 1/8"   B. 3'2 1/2"   C. 3'3 1/4"   D. 3'3 5/8"

4. According to the building code, the MAXIMUM permitted surface temperature of combustible construction materials located near heating equipment is 76.5°C. (°F=(°Cx9/5)+32)
   Maximum temperature Fahrenheit is MOST NEARLY   4._____

   A. 170° F   B. 195° F   C. 210° F   D. 220° F

5. A pump discharges 7.5 gals/minutes.
   In 2.5 hours the pump will discharge _____ gallons.   5._____

   A. 1125   B. 1875   C. 1950   D. 2200

6. A pipe with an outside diameter of 4" has a circumference of MOST NEARLY _____ inches.   6._____

   A. 8.05   B. 9.81   C. 12.57   D. 14.92

7. A piping sketch is drawn to a scale of 1/8" = 1 foot.
   A vertical steam line measuring 3 1/2" on the sketch would have an ACTUAL length of _____ feet.   7._____

   A. 16   B. 22   C. 24   D. 28

8. A pipe having an inside diameter of 3.48 inches and a wall thickness of .18 inches will have an outside diameter of _____ inches.   8._____

   A. 3.84   B. 3.64   C. 3.57   D. 3.51

9. A rectangular steel bar having a volume of 30 cubic inches, a width of 2 inches, and a height of 3 inches will have a length of _____ inches.   9._____

   A. 12   B. 10   C. 8   D. 5

10. A pipe weighs 20.4 pounds per foot of length.
    The total weight of eight pieces of this pipe with each piece 20 feet in length is MOST NEARLY _____ pounds.   10._____

    A. 460   B. 1,680   C. 2,420   D. 3,260

11. Assume that four pieces of pipe measuring 2'1 1/4", 4'2 3/4", 5'1 9/16", and 6'3 5/8", respectively, are cut with a saw from a pipe 20'0" long.
    Allowing 1/16" waste for each cut, the length of the remaining pipe is

    A. 2'1 9/16"   B. 2'2 9/16"   C. 2'4 13/16"   D. 2'8 9/16"

12. If one cubic inch of steel weighs 0.28 pounds, the weight, in pounds, of a steel bar 1/2" x 6" x 2'0" long is MOST NEARLY

    A. 11   B. 16   C. 20   D. 24

13. If the circumference of a circle is equal to 31.416 inches, then its diameter, in inches, is equal to MOST NEARLY

    A. 8   B. 9   C. 10   D. 13

14. Assume that a steam fitter's helper receives a salary of $171.36 a day for 250 days is considered a full work year. If taxes, social security, hospitalization, and pension deducted from his salary amounts to 16 percent of his gross pay, then his net yearly salary will be MOST NEARLY

    A. $31,788   B. $35,982   C. $41,982   D. $42,840

15. If the outside diameter of a pipe is 14 inches and the wall thickness is 1/2 inch, then the inside area of the pipe, in square inches, is MOST NEARLY

    A. 125   B. 133   C. 143   D. 154

16. A steam leak in a pipe line allows steam to escape at a rate of 50,000 pounds each month.
    Assuming that the cost of steam is $2.50 per 1,000 pounds, the TOTAL cost of wasted steam from this leak for a 12-month period would amount to

    A. $125   B. $300   C. $1,500   D. $3,000

17. If 250 feet of 4" pipe weighs 400 pounds, the weight of this pipe per linear foot is _____ pounds.

    A. 1.25   B. 1.50   C. 1.60   D. 1.75

18. A set of heating plan drawings is drawn to a scale of 1/4" = 1 foot.
    If a length of pipe measures 4 5/8" on the drawing, the ACTUAL length of the pipe, in feet, is

    A. 16.3   B. 16.8   C. 17.5   D. 18.5

19. The TOTAL length of four pieces of pipe whose lengths are 3'4 1/2", 2'1 5/16", 4'9 3/8", and 2'3 1/4", respectively, is

    A. 11'5 7/16"   B. 11'6 7/16"
    C. 12'5 7/16"   D. 12'6 7/16"

20. Assume that a pipe trench is 3 feet wide, 3 feet deep, and 300 feet long.
    If the unit cost of excavating the trench is $120 per cubic yard, the TOTAL cost of excavating the trench is

    A. $1,200   B. $12,000   C. $27,000   D. $36,000

21. The TOTAL length of four pieces of 1 1/2" galvanized steel pipe whose lengths are 7 ft. + 3 1/2 inches, 4 ft. + 2 1/4 inches, 6 ft. + 7 inches, and 8 ft. +5 1/8 inches is

    A. 26 feet + 5 7/8 inches
    B. 25 ft. + 6 7/8 inches
    C. 25 feet + 4 1/4 inches
    D. 25 ft. + 3 3/8 inches

22. A swimming pool is 25' wide by 75' long and has an average depth of 5'. 1 cubic foot contains 7.5 gallons of water. The capacity, when filled to the overflow, is _____ gallons.

    A. 9,375
    B. 65,625
    C. 69,005
    D. 70,312

23. The sum of 3 1/4, 5 1/8, 2 1/2 , and 3 3/8 is

    A. 14
    B. 14 1/8
    C. 14 1/4
    D. 14 3/8

24. Assume that it takes 6 men 8 days to do a particular job. If you have only 4 men available to do this job and they all work at the same speed, then the number of days it would take to complete the job would be

    A. 11
    B. 12
    C. 13
    D. 14

25. The total length of four pieces of 2" O.D. pipe, whose lengths are 7'3 1/2", 4'2 3/16", 5'7 5/16", and 8'5 7/8", respectively, is MOST NEARLY

    A. 24'6 3/4"
    B. 24'7 15/16"
    C. 25'5 13/16"
    D. 25'6 7/8"

KEY (CORRECT ANSWERS)

1.	C	11.	B
2.	C	12.	C
3.	D	13.	C
4.	A	14.	B
5.	A	15.	B
6.	C	16.	C
7.	D	17.	C
8.	A	18.	D
9.	D	19.	D
10.	D	20.	B

21. A
22. D
23. C
24. B
25. D

SOLUTIONS TO PROBLEMS

1. 15 5/8" + 8 3/4" + 30 5/16" + 20 1/2" = 73 35/16" = 75 3/16"

2. Inside diameter = 6" - 1/2" - 1/2" = 5". Area = $(\pi)(5/2")^2 \approx$ 19.6 sq. in.

3. Pipe remaining = 14' - 1'10" - 3'2 1/2" - 5'7 1/2" - (3)(1/8") = 3'3 5/8"

4. 76.5 x 9/5 = 137.7 + 32 = 169.7

5. 7.5 x 150 = 1125

6. Radius = 2" Circumference = $(2\pi)(2") \approx$ 12.57"

7. 3 1/2" 1/8" = (7/2)(8/1) = 28 Then, (28)(1 ft.) = 28 feet

8. Outside diameter = 3.48" + .18" + .18" = 3.84"

9. 30 = (2)(3)(length). So, length = 5"

10. Total weight = (20.4)(8)(20) $\approx$ 3260 lbs.

11. 20' - 2'1 1/4" - 4'2 3/4" - 5'1 9/16" - 6'3 5/8" - (4)(1/16") = 2'2 9/16"

12. Weight = (.28)(1/2")(6")(24") = 20.16 $\approx$ 20 lbs.

13. Diameter = 31.416" $\div \pi \approx$ 10"

14. His net pay for 250 days = (.84)($171.36)(250) = $35,985.60 $\approx$ $35,928 (from answer key)

15. Inside diameter = 14" - 1/2" - 1/2" = 13". Area = $(\pi)(13/2")^2 \approx$ 133 sq.in

16. (50,000 lbs.)(12) = 600,000 lbs. per year. The cost would be ($2.50)(600) = $1500

17. 400 $\div$ 250 = 1.60 pounds per linear foot

18. 4 5/8" $\div$ 1/4" = 37/8 . 4/1 = 18.5 Then, (18.5)(1 ft.) = 18.5 feet

19. 3'4 1/2" + 2'1 5/16" + 4'9 3/8" + 2'3 1/4" = 11'17 23/16" = 12'6 7/16"

20. (3')(3')(300') = 2700 cu.ft., which is 2700 $\div$ 27 = 100 cu.yds. Total cost = ($120)(100) = $12,000

21. 7'3 1/2" + 4'2 1/4" + 6'7" + 8'5 1/8" = 25'17 7/8" = 26'5 7/8"

22. (25)(75)(5) = 9375 cu.ft. Then, (9375)(7.5) $\approx$ 70,312 gals.

23. 3 1/4 + 5 1/8 + 2 1/2 + 3 3/8 = 13 10/8 = 14 1/4

24. (6) (8) = 48 man-days. Then, 48 $\div$ 4 = 12 days

25. 7'3 1/2" + 4'2 3/16" + 5'7 5/16" + 8'5 7/8"= 24'17 30/16" = 25'6 7/8"

TEST 3

DIRECTIONS: Each question or incomplete statement is followed by several suggested answers or completions. Select the one that BEST answers the question or completes the statement. *PRINT THE LETTER OF THE CORRECT ANSWER IN THE SPACE AT THE RIGHT.*

1. The time required to pump 2,500 gallons of water out of a sump at the rate of 12 1/2 gallons per minutes would be _____ hour(s) _____ minutes.   1._____

   A. 1; 40   B. 2; 30   C. 3; 20   D. 6; 40

2. Copper tubing which has an inside diameter of 1 1/16" and a wall thickness of .095" has an outside diameter which is MOST NEARLY _____ inches.   2._____

   A. 1 5/32   B. 1 3/16   C. 1 7/32   D. 1 1/4

3. Assume that 90 gallons per minute flow through a certain 3-inch pipe which is tapped into a street main.
   The amount of water which would flow through a 1-inch pipe tapped into the same street main is MOST NEARLY _____ gpm.   3._____

   A. 90   B. 45   C. 30   D. 10

4. The weight of a 6 foot length of 8-inch pipe which weighs 24.70 pounds per foot is _____ lbs.   4._____

   A. 148.2   B. 176.8   C. 197.6   D. 212.4

5. If a 4-inch pipe is directly coupled to a 2-inch pipe and 16 gallons per minute are flowing through the 4-inch pipe, then the flow through the 2-inch pipe will be _____ gallons per minute.   5._____

   A. 4   B. 8   C. 16   D. 32

6. If the water pressure at the bottom of a column of water 34 feet high is 14.7 pounds per square inch, the water pressure at the bottom of a column of water 18 feet high is MOST NEARLY _____ pounds per square inch.   6._____

   A. 8.0   B. 7.8   C. 7.6   D. 7.4

7. If there are 7 1/2 gallons in a cubic foot of water and if water flows from a hose at a constant rate of 4 gallons per minute, the time it should take to COMPLETELY fill a tank of 1,600 cubic feet capacity with water from that hose is _____ hours.   7._____

   A. 300   B. 150   C. 100   D. 50

8. Each of a group of fifteen water meter readers read an average of 62 water meters a day in a certain 5-day work week. A total of 5,115 meters are read by this group the following week.
   The TOTAL number of meters read in the second week as compared to the first week shows a   8._____

   A. 10% increase   B. 15% increase
   C. 20% increase   D. 5% decrease

9. A certain water consumer used 5% more water in 1994 than he did in 1993. If his water consumption for 1994 was 8,375 cubic feet, the amount of water he consumed in 1993 was MOST NEARLY _____ cubic feet.

   A. 9,014   B. 8,816   C. 7,976   D. 6,776

10. Assume that a water meter reads 40,175 cubic feet and that the previous reading was 29,186 cubic feet.
    If the charge for water is 92 cents per 100 cubic feet or any fraction thereof, the bill for the amount of water used since the previous meter reading should be

    A. $100.28   B. $101.04   C. $101.08   D. $101.20

11. A leaking faucet caused a loss of 216 cubic feet of water in a 30-day month. If there are 7.5 gallons in a cubic foot of water, then the AVERAGE loss of water per hour for that month was _____ gallons.

    A. 2 1/4   B. 2 1/8   C. 2   D. 1 3/4

12. The fraction which is equal to .375 is

    A. 3/16   B. 5/32   C. 3/8   D. 5/12

13. A square backyard swimming pool, each side of which is 10 feet long, is filled to a depth of 3 1/2 feet.
    If there are 7 1/2 gallons in a cubic foot of water, the number of gallons of water in the pool is MOST NEARLY _____ gallons.

    A. 46.7   B. 100   C. 2,625   D. 3,500

14. When 1 5/8, 3 3/4, 6 1/3, and 9 1/2 are added, the resulting sum is

    A. 21 1/8   B. 21 1/6   C. 21 5/24   D. 21 1/4

15. When 946 1/2 is subtracted from 1,035 1/4, the result is

    A. 87 1/4   B. 87 3/4   C. 88 1/4   D. 88 3/4

16. When 39 is multiplied by 697, the result is

    A. 8,364   B. 26,283   C. 27,183   D. 28,003

17. When 16.074 is divided by .045, the result is

    A. 3.6   B. 35.7   C. 357.2   D. 3,572

18. To dig a trench 3'0" wide, 50'0" long, and 5'6" deep, the total number of cubic yards of earth to be removed is MOST NEARLY

    A. 30   B. 90   C. 140   D. 825

19. The TOTAL length of four pieces of 2" pipe, whose lengths are 7'3 1/2", 4'2 3/16", 5'7 5/16", and 8'5 7/8", respectively, is

    A. 24'6 3/4"   B. 24'7 15/16"
    C. 25'5 13/16"   D. 25'6 7/8"

20. A hot water line made of copper has a straight horizontal run of 150 feet and, when installed, is at a temperature of 45° F. In use, its temperature rises to 190° F.
If the coefficient of expansion for copper is 0.0000095" per foot per degree F, the TOTAL expansion, in inches, in the run of pipe is given by the product of 150 multiplied by 0.0000095 by

   A. 145
   B. 145 x 12
   C. 145 divided by 12
   D. 145 x 12 x 12

21. A water storage tank measures 5' long, 4' wide, and 6' deep and is filled to the 5 1/2' mark with water.
If one cubic foot of water weighs 62 pounds, the number of pounds of water required to COMPLETELY fill the tank is

   A. 7,440   B. 6,200   C. 1,240   D. 620

22. Assume that a pipe worker earns $83,125.00 per year.
If seventeen percent of his pay is deducted for taxes, social security, and pension, his net weekly pay will be APPROXIMATELY

   A. $1598.50   B. $1504.00   C. $1453.00   D. $1325.00

23. If eighteen feet of 4" cast iron pipe weighs approximately 390 pounds, the weight of this pipe per lineal foot will be MOST NEARLY _____ lbs.

   A. 19   B. 22   C. 23   D. 25

24. If it takes 3 men 11 days to dig a trench, the number of days it will take 5 men to dig the same trench, assuming all work is done at the same rate of speed, is MOST NEARLY

   A. 6 1/2   B. 7 3/4   C. 8 1/4   D. 8 3/4

25. If a trench is dug 6'0" deep, 2'6" wide, and 8'0" long, the area of the opening, in square feet, is MOST NEARLY

   A. 48   B. 32   C. 20   D. 15

KEY (CORRECT ANSWERS)

1.	C	11.	A
2.	D	12.	C
3.	D	13.	C
4.	A	14.	C
5.	B	15.	D
6.	B	16.	C
7.	D	17.	C
8.	A	18.	A
9.	C	19.	D
10.	D	20.	A

21. D
22. D
23. B
24. A
25. C

5 (#3)

SOLUTIONS TO PROBLEMS

1. 2500 ÷ 12 1/2 = 200 min. = 3 hrs. 20 min.

2. 1 1/16" + .095" + .095" = 1.0625 + .095 + .095 = 1.2525" ≈ 1 1/4"

3. Cross-sectional areas for a 3-inch pipe and a 1-inch pipe are $(\pi)(1.5)^2$ and $(\pi)(.5)^2$ = 2.25π and $.25\pi$, respectively. Let x = amount of water flowing through the 1-inch pipe. Then, $\frac{90}{x} = \frac{2.25\pi}{.25\pi}$. Solving, x = 10 gals/min

4. (24.70)(6) = 148.2 lbs.

5. $\frac{4" \text{ pipe}}{16 \text{ gallons}} = \frac{2" \text{ pipe}}{x \text{ gallons}}$, 4x = 32, x = 8

6. Let x = pressure. Then, 34/18 = 14.7/x. Solving, x ≈ 7.8

7. (1600)(7.5) = 12,000 gallons. Then, 12,000 ÷ 4 = 3000 min. = 50 hours

8. (15)(62)(5) = 4650. Then, (5115-4650)/4650 = 10% increase

9. 8375 ÷ 1.05 ≈ 7976 cu.ft.

10. 40,175 - 29,186 = 10,989 cu.ft. Then, 10,989 100 = 109.89. Since .92 is charged for each 100 cu.ft. or fraction thereof, total cost = (.92)(110) = $101.20

11. (216)(7.5) = 1620 gallons. In 30 days, there are 720 hours. Thus, the average water loss per hour = 1620 ÷ 720 = 2 1/4 gallons.

12. .375 = 375/1000 = 3/8

13. Volume = (10)(10)(3 1/2) = 350 cu.ft. Then, (350)(7 1/2) = 2625 gallons

14. 1 5/8 + 3 3/4 + 6 1/3 + 9 1/2 = 19 53/24 = 21 5/24

15. 1035 1/4 - 946 1/2 = 88 3/4

16. (39)(697) = 27,183

17. 16.074 .045 = 357.2

18. (3')(50')(5 1/2') = 825 cu.ft. ≈ 30 cu.yds., since 1 cu.yd. = 27 cu.ft.

19. 7'3 1/2" + 4'2 3/16" + 5'7 5/16" + 8'5 7/8" = 24'17 30/16" = 25'6 7/8"

20. Total expansion = (150)(.0000095)(145)

21. Number of pounds needed = (5)(4)(6-5 1/2)(62) = 620

22. Net annual pay = ($83,125)(.83) ≈ $69000. Then, the net weekly pay = $69000 ÷ 52 ≈ $1325 (actually about $1327)

23. 390 lbs. ÷ 18 = 21.6 lbs. per linear foot

24. (3)(11) = 33 man-days. Then, 33 ÷ 5 = 6.6 ≈ 6 1/2 days

25. Area = (8')(2 1/2') = 20 sq.ft.

ARITHMETICAL REASONING

EXAMINATION SECTION
TEST 1

DIRECTIONS: Each question or incomplete statement is followed by several suggested answers or completions. Select the one that BEST answers the question or completes the statement. *PRINT THE LETTER OF THE CORRECT ANSWER IN THE SPACE AT THE RIGHT.*

1. If it takes 2 men 9 days to do a job, how many men are needed to do the same job in 3 days?

    A. 4   B. 5   C. 6   D. 7

2. Suppose that a department operates 1,644 buildings. If one employee is needed for every 2 buildings, and one foreman is needed for every 18 employees, the number of foremen needed is CLOSEST to

    A. 45   B. 50   C. 55   D. 60

3. If 60 bars of soap cost the same as 2 gallons of wax, how many bars of soap can be bought for the price of 5 gallons of wax?

    A. 120   B. 150   C. 180   D. 300

4. An employee waxes 275 sq.ft. of floor on Monday, 352 sq.ft. on Tuesday, 179 sq.ft. on Wednesday, and 302 sq.ft. on Thursday.
    In order to average 280 sq.ft. of floor waxed a day, how many square feet of floor must he wax on Friday?

    A. 264   B. 278   C. 292   D. 358

5. A project covers 35 acres altogether. Lawns, playgrounds, and walks take up 28 acres and the rest is given over to buildings.
    What percentage of the total area is given over to buildings?

    A. 7%   B. 20%   C. 25%   D. 28%

6. When preparing for a mopping operation, fill the standard 16 quart bucket to the 3/4 full mark with warm water. Then add detergent at the rate of 2 oz. per gallon of water and disinfectant at the rate of 1 oz. to 3 gallons of water. According to these directions, the amount of detergent and disinfectant to add to 3/4 of a bucket of warm water is _____ oz. detergent and _____ oz. disinfectant.

    A. 4; 1/2   B. 5; 3/4   C. 6; 1   D. 8; 1 1/4

7. If corn brooms weigh 32 lbs. a dozen, the average weight of one corn broom is CLOSEST to _____ lbs. _____ oz.

    A. 2; 14   B. 2; 11   C. 2; 9   D. 2; 6

8. At the beginning of the year, a foreman has 7 dozen electric bulbs in stock. During the year, he receives a shipment of 14 dozen bulbs, and also replaces 5 burned out bulbs a month in each of 3 buildings in his area. How many electric bulbs does he have on hand at the end of the year? _____ dozen.

   A. 3   B. 6   C. 8   D. 12

9. A project has 4 buildings, each 14 floors high. Each floor has 10 apartments. If 35% of the apartments in the project have 3 rooms or less, how many apartments have 4 or more rooms?

   A. 196   B. 210   C. 364   D. 406

10. An employee takes 1 hour and 30 minutes a day to sweep 30 flights of stairs. How many flights of stairs does he sweep in a month if he spends a total of 30 hours doing this job and works at the same rate?

    A. 200   B. 300   C. 600   D. 900

11. During a month, Employee A washed 30 windows, Employee B washed 4 times as many windows as Employee A, and Employee C washed half as many windows as Employee B. The TOTAL number of windows washed by all three men together during this month is

    A. 180   B. 210   C. 240   D. 330

12. How much would it cost to completely fence in the playground area shown at the right with fencing costing $7.50 a foot?
    A. $615.00
    B. $820.00
    C. $885.00
    D. $960.00

13. A drill bit measures .625 inches. The fractional equivalent, in inches, is

    A. 9/16   B. 5/8   C. 11/16   D. 3/4

14. The number of cubic yards of sand required to fill a bin measuring 12 feet by 6 feet by 4 feet is MOST NEARLY

    A. 8   B. 11   C. 48   D. 96

15. Assume that you are assigned to put down floor tiles in a room measuring 8 feet by 10 feet. Individual tiles measure 9 inches by 9 inches.
    The total number of floor tiles required to cover the entire floor is MOST NEARLY

    A. 107   B. 121   C. 142   D. 160

16. Lumber is usually sold by the board foot, and a board foot is defined as a board one foot square and one inch thick.
    If the price of one board foot of lumber is 90 cents and you need 20 feet of lumber 6 inches wide and 1 inch thick, the cost of the 20 feet of lumber is

    A. $9.00   B. $12.00   C. $18.00   D. $24.00

17. For a certain plumbing repair job, you need three lengths of pipe, 12 1/4 inches, 6 1/2 inches, and 8 5/8 inches.
    If you cut these three lengths from the same piece of pipe, which is 36 inches long, and each cut consumes 1/8 inch of pipe, the length of pipe REMAINING after you have cut out your three pieces should be _____ inches.

    A. 7 1/4   B. 7 7/8   C. 8 1/4   D. 8 7/8

18. A maintenance bond for a roadway pavement is in an amount of 10% of the estimated cost.
    If the estimated cost is $8,000,000, the maintenance bond is

    A. $8,000   B. $80,000   C. $800,000   D. $8,000,000

19. Specifications require that a core be taken every 700 square yards of paved roadway or fraction thereof. A 100 foot by 200 foot rectangular area would require _____ core(s).

    A. 1   B. 2   C. 3   D. 4

20. An applicant must file a map at a scale of 1" = 40'. Six inches on the map represents _____ feet on the ground.

    A. 600   B. 240   C. 120   D. 60

21. A 100' x 110' lot has an area of MOST NEARLY _____ acre.

    A. 1/8   B. 1/4   C. 3/8   D. 1/2

22. 1 inch is MOST NEARLY equal to _____ feet.

    A. .02   B. .04   C. .06   D. .08

23. The area of the triangle EFG shown at the right is MOST NEARLY _____ sq. ft.

    A. 36   B. 42   C. 48   D. 54

24. Specifications state: As further security for the faithful performance of this contract, the Comptroller shall deduct, and retain until the final payment, 10% of the value of the work certified for payment in each partial payment voucher, until the amount so deducted and retained shall equal 5% of the contract price or in the case of a unit price contract, 5% of the estimated amount to be paid to the Contractor under the contract.
    For a $300,000 contract, the amount to be retained at the end of the contract is

    A. $5,000   B. $10,000   C. $15,000   D. $20,000

25. Asphalt was laid for a length of 210 feet on the entire width of a street whose curb-to-curb distance is 30 feet. The number of square yards covered with asphalt is MOST NEARLY

    A. 210   B. 700   C. 2,100   D. 6,300

KEY (CORRECT ANSWERS)

1.	C	11.	B
2.	A	12.	C
3.	B	13.	B
4.	C	14.	B
5.	B	15.	C
6.	C	16.	A
7.	B	17.	C
8.	B	18.	C
9.	C	19.	D
10.	C	20.	B

21. B
22. D
23. A
24. C
25. B

SOLUTIONS TO PROBLEMS

1. (2)(9) = 18 man-days. Then, 18 ÷ 3 = 6 men

2. The number of employees = 1644 ÷ 2 = 822. The number of foremen needed = 822 ÷ 18 ≈ 45

3. 1 gallon of wax costs the same as 60 ÷ 2 = 30 bars of soap. Thus, 5 gallons of wax costs the same as (5)(30) = 150 bars of soap.

4. To average 280 sq.ft. for five days means a total of (5)(280) = 1400 sq.ft. for all five days. The number of square feet to be waxed on Friday = 1400 - (275+352+179+302) = 292

5. The acreage for buildings is 35 - 28 = 7. Then, 7/35 = 20%

6. (16)(3/4) = 12 quarts = 3 gallons. The amount of detergent, in ounces, is (2)(3) = 6. The amount of disinfectant is 1 oz.

7. One corn broom weighs 32 ÷ 12 = 2 2/3 lbs. ≈ 2 lbs. 11 oz.

8. Number of bulbs at the beginning of the year = (7)(12) + (14)(12) = 252. Number of bulbs replaced over an entire year = (5)(3)(12) = 180. The number of unused bulbs = 252 - 180 = 72 = 6 dozen.

9. Total number of apartments = (4)(14)(10) = 560. The number of apartments with at least 4 rooms = (.65)(560) = 364.

10. 30 ÷ 1 1/2 = 20. Then, (20)(30) = 600 flights of stairs

11. The number of windows washed by A, B, C were 30, 120, and 60. Their total is 210.

12. The two missing dimensions are 26 - 14 = 12 ft. and 33 - 9 = 24 ft. Perimeter = 9 + 12 + 33 + 26 + 24 + 14 = 118 ft. Thus, total cost of fencing = (118)($7.50) = $885.00

13. $.625 = \dfrac{625}{1000} = \dfrac{5}{8}$

14. (12)(6)(4) = 288 cu.ft. Now, 1 cu.yd. = 27 cu.ft.; 288 cu.ft. is equivalent to 10 2/3 or about 11 cu.yds.

15. 144 sq.in. = 1 sq.ft. The room measures (8 ft.)x(10 ft.) = 80 sq.ft. = 11,520 sq.in. Each tile measures (9)(9) = 81 sq.in. The number of tiles needed = 11,520 ÷ 81 = 142.2 or about 142.

16. 20 ft. by 6 in. = (20 ft.)(1/2 ft.) = 10 sq.ft. Then, (10X.90) = $9.00

17. There will be 3 cuts in making 3 lengths of pipe, and these 3 cuts will use (3)(1/8) = 3/8 in. of pipe. The amount of pipe remaining after the 3 pieces are removed = 36 - 12 1/4 - 6 1/2 - 8 5/8 - 3/8 = 8 1/4 in.

18. The maintenance bond = (.10)($8,000,000) = $800,000

19. $(100)(200) = 20,000$ sq.ft. $= 20,000 \div 9 \approx 2222$ sq.yds. Then, $2222 \div 700 \approx 3.17$. Since a core must be taken for each 700 sq.yds. plus any left over fraction, 4 cores will be needed.

20. Six inches means $(6)(40) = 240$ ft. of actual length.

21. $(100 \text{ ft.})(110 \text{ ft.}) = 11,000$ sq.ft. ≈ 1222 sq.yds. Then, since 1 acre $= 4840$ sq.yds., 1222 sq.yds. is equivalent to about 1/4 acre.

22. 1 in. $= 1/12$ ft. $\approx .08$ ft.

23. Area of $\triangle EFG = (1/2)(8)(6) + (1/2)(4)(6) = 36$ sq.ft.

24. The amount to be retained $= (.05)(\$300,000) = \$15,000$

25. $(210)(30) = 6300$ sq.ft. Since 1 sq.yd. $= 9$ sq.ft., 6300 sq.ft. equals 700 sq.yds.

TEST 2

DIRECTIONS: Each question or incomplete statement is followed by several suggested answers or completions. Select the one that BEST answers the question or completes the statement. *PRINT THE LETTER OF THE CORRECT ANSWER IN THE SPACE AT THE RIGHT.*

1. The TOTAL length of four pieces of 2" pipe, whose lengths are 7'3 1/2", 4'2 3/16", 5'7 5/16", and 8'5 7/8", respectively, is

    A. 24'6 3/4"
    B. 24'7 15/16"
    C. 25'5 13/16"
    D. 25'6 7/8"

2. Under the same conditions, the group of pipes that gives the SAME flow as one 6" pipe is (neglecting friction) _____ pipes.

    A. 3 3" B. 4 3" C. 2 4" D. 3 4"

3. A water storage tank measures 5' long, 4' wide, and 6' deep and is filled to the 5 1/2' mark with water.
If one cubic foot of water weighs 62 pounds, the number of pounds of water required to COMPLETELY fill the tank is

    A. 7,440 B. 6,200 C. 1,240 D. 620

4. A hot water line made of copper has a straight horizontal run of 150 feet and, when installed, is at a temperature of 45°F. In use, its temperature rises to 190°F.
If the coefficient of expansion for copper is 0.0000095" per foot per degree F, the total expansion, in inches, in the run of pipe is given by the product of 150 multiplied by 0.0000095 by

    A. 145
    B. 145 x 12
    C. 145 divided by 12
    D. 145 x 12 x 12

5. To dig a trench 3'0" wide, 50'0" long, and 5'6" deep, the total number of cubic yards of earth to be removed is MOST NEARLY

    A. 30 B. 90 C. 140 D. 825

6. If it costs $65 for 20 feet of subway rail, the cost of 150 feet of this rail will be

    A. $487.50 B. $512.00 C. $589.50 D. $650.00

7. The number of cubic feet of concrete it takes to fill a form 10 feet long, 3 feet wide, and 6 inches deep is

    A. 12 B. 15 C. 20 D. 180

8. The sum of 4 1/16, 5 1/4, 3 5/8, and 4 7/16 is

    A. 17 3/16 B. 17 1/4 C. 17 5/16 D. 17 3/8

9. If you earn $10.20 per hour and time and one-half for working over 40 hours, your gross salary for a week in which you worked 42 hours would be

    A. $408.00 B. $428.40 C. $438.60 D. $770.80

41

2 (#2)

10. A drill bit, used to drill holes in track ties, has a diameter of 0.75 inches. When expressed as a fraction, the diameter of this drill bit is

   A. 1/4" B. 3/8" C. 1/2" D. 3/4"

11. Three dozen shovels were purchased for use.
    If the shovels were used at the rate of nine a week, the number of weeks that the three dozen lasted was

   A. 3 B. 4 C. 9 D. 12

12. Assume that you earn $20,000 per year.
    If twenty percent of your pay is deducted for taxes, social security, and pension, your weekly take-home pay will be MOST NEARLY

   A. $280 B. $308 C. $328 D. $344

13. If a measurement scaled from a drawing is one inch, and the scale of the drawing is 1/8 inch to the foot, then the one inch measurement would represent an ACTUAL length of

   A. 8 feet
   C. 1/8 of a foot
   B. 2 feet
   D. 8 inches

14. Tiles 12" x 12" are used to lay a floor having the dimensions 10'0" x 12'0". The MINIMUM number of tiles needed to completely cover the floor is

   A. 60 B. 96 C. 120 D. 144

15. The volume of concrete in a strip of sidewalk 30 feet long by 4 feet wide by 3 inches thick is _____ cubic feet.

   A. 30 B. 120 C. 240 D. 360

16. To change a quantity of cubic feet into an equivalent quantity of cubic yards, _____ the quantity by _____.

   A. multiply; 9
   C. multiply; 27
   B. divide; 9
   D. divide; 27

17. If a pump can deliver 50 gallons of water per minute, then the time needed for this pump to empty an excavation containing 5,800 gallons of water is _____ hour(s) _____ minutes.

   A. 2; 12 B. 1; 56 C. 1; 44 D. 1; 32

18. The sum of 3 1/6", 4 1/4", 3 5/8", and 5 7/16" is

   A. 15 9/16" B. 16 1/8" C. 16 23/48" D. 16 3/4"

19. If a measurement scaled from a drawing is 2 inches, and the scale of the drawing is 1/8 inch to the foot, then the two inch measurement would represent an ACTUAL length of

   A. 8 feet
   C. 1/4 of a foot
   B. 4 feet
   D. 16 feet

20. A room is 7'6" wide by 9'0" long with a ceiling height of 8'0". One gallon of flat paint will cover approximately 400 square feet of wall.
    The number of gallons of this paint required to paint the walls of this room, making no deductions for windows or doors, is MOST NEARLY

    A. 1/4   B. 1/2   C. 2/3   D. 1

21. The cost of a certain job is broken down as follows:

    Materials $3,750
    Rental of equipment 1,200
    Labor   3,150

    The percentage of the total cost of the job that can be charged to materials is MOST NEARLY

    A. 40%   B. 42%   C. 44%   D. 46%

22. By trial, it is found that by using two cubic feet of sand, a 5 cubic foot batch of concrete is produced. Using the same proportions, the amount of sand required to produce 2 cubic yards of concrete is MOST NEARLY _____ cubic feet.

    A. 20   B. 22   C. 24   D. 26

23. It takes 4 men 6 days to do a certain job.
    Working at the same speed, the number of days it will take 3 men to do this job is

    A. 7   B. 8   C. 9   D. 10

24. The cost of rawl plugs is $27.50 per gross. The cost of 2,448 rawl plugs is

    A. $467.50   B. $472.50   C. $477.50   D. $482.50

25. In a certain district, the area of a building may be no longer than 55% of the area of the lot on which it stands. On a rectangular lot 75 ft. by 125 ft., the maximum permissible area of building is, in square feet, MOST NEARLY

    A. 5,148   B. 5,152   C. 5,156   D. 5,160

KEY (CORRECT ANSWERS)

1.	D	11.	B
2.	B	12.	B
3.	D	13.	A
4.	A	14.	C
5.	A	15.	A
6.	A	16.	D
7.	B	17.	B
8.	D	18.	C
9.	C	19.	D
10.	D	20.	C

21. D
22. B
23. B
24. A
25. C

5 (#2)

SOLUTIONS TO PROBLEMS

1. $3\frac{1}{6}" + 4\frac{1}{4}" + 3\frac{5}{8}" + 5\frac{7}{16}" = 3\frac{8}{48}" + 4\frac{12}{48}" + 3\frac{30}{48}" + 5\frac{21}{48}" = 15\frac{71}{48}" = 16\frac{23}{48}"$

2. The flow of a 6" pipe is measured by the cross-sectional area. Since diameter = 6", radius = 3", and so area = 9 π sq.in. A single 3" pipe would have a cross-sectional area of (3/2) π sq.in. = 2.25 π sq.in. Now, 9 ÷ / 2.25 = 4. Thus, four 3" pipes is equivalent, in flow, to one 6" pipe.

3. (5x4x6) - (5x4x5 1/2) = 10. Then, (10)(62) = 620 pounds.

4. The total expansion = (150')(.0000095"/1 ft.)(190°-45°). So, the last factor is 145.

5. (3')(50')(5 1/2') = 825 cu.ft. Since 1 cu.yd. = 27 cu.ft., 825 cu.ft. cu.yds.

6. 150 ÷ 20 = 7.5. Then, (7.5)($65) = $487.50

7. (10')(3')(1/2') = 15 cu.ft.

8. $4\frac{1}{16} + 5\frac{4}{16} + 3\frac{10}{16} + 4\frac{7}{16} = 16\frac{22}{16} = 17\frac{3}{8}$

9. Gross salary = ($10.20)(40) + ($15.30)(2) = $438.60

10. $75" = \frac{75}{100}" = \frac{3}{4}"$

11. 3 dozen = 36 shovels. Then, 36 ÷ 9 = 4 weeks

12. Since 20% is deducted, the take-home pay = ($20,000)(.80) = $16,000 for the year, which is $16,000 ÷ 52 ≈ $308 per week.

13. A scale drawing where 1/8" means an actual size of 1 ft. implies that a scale drawing of 1" means an actual size of (1')(8) = 8'

14. (10')(12') = 120 sq.ft. Since each tile is 1 sq.ft., a total of 120 tiles will be used.

15. (30')(4')(1/4') = 30 cu.ft.

16. To convert a given number of cubic feet into an equivalent number of cubic yards, divide by 27.

17. 5800 ÷ 50 = 116 min. = 1 hour 56 minutes

18. $3\frac{1}{6}" + 4\frac{1}{4}" + 3\frac{5}{8}" + 5\frac{7}{16}" = 3\frac{8}{48}" + 4\frac{12}{48}" + 3\frac{30}{48}" + 5\frac{21}{48}" = 15\frac{71}{48}" = 16\frac{23}{48}"$

19. 2 ÷ 1/8 = 16, so a 2" drawing represents an actual length of 16 feet.

6 (#2)

20. The area of the 4 walls = 2(7 1/2')(8') + 2(9')(8') = 264 sq.ft. Then, 264 ÷ 400 = .66 or about 2/3 gallon of paint.

21. $3750 + $1200 + $3150 = $8100. Then, $3750/$8100 ≈ 46%

22. 2 cu.yds. ÷ 5 cu.ft. = 54 ÷ 5 = 10.8. Now, (10.8)(2 cu.ft.) ≈ 22 cu.ft. Note: 2 cu.yds. = 54 cu.ft.

23. (4)(6) = 24 man-days. Then, 24 ÷ 3 = 8 days

24. 2448 ÷ 144 = 17. Then, (17)($27.50) = $467.50

25. (75')(125') = 9375 sq.ft. The maximum area of the building = (.55)(9375 sq.ft.) ≈ 5156 sq.ft.

———

TEST 3

DIRECTIONS: Each question or incomplete statement is followed by several suggested answers or completions. Select the one that BEST answers the question or completes the statement. *PRINT THE LETTER OF THE CORRECT ANSWER IN THE SPACE AT THE RIGHT.*

1. A steak weighed 2 pounds, 4 ounces. How much did it cost at $4.60 per pound?   1.____
   A. $7.80   B. $8.75   C. $9.90   D. $10.35

2. twenty pints of water just fill a pail. the capacity of the pail, in gallons, is   2.____
   A. 2   B. 2 1/4   C. 2 1/2   D. 2 3/4

3. The sum of 5/12 and 1/4 is   3.____
   A. 7/12   B. 2/3   C. 3/4   D. 5/6

4. The volume of earth, in cubic yards, excavated from a trench 4'0" wide by 5'6" deep by 18'6" long is MOST NEARLY   4.____
   A. 14.7   B. 15.1   C. 15.5   D. 15.9

5. 5/8 written as a decimal is   5.____
   A. 62.5   B. 6.25   C. .625   D. .0625

6. The number of cubic feet in a cubic yard is   6.____
   A. 9   B. 12   C. 27   D. 36

7. If it costs $16.20 to lay one square yard of asphalt, to lay a patch 15' by 15', it will cost MOST NEARLY   7.____
   A. $405.00   B. $3,645.00   C. $134.50   D. $243.00

8. You are assigned thirty (30) asphalt workers to be divided into two crews so that one crew will have 2/3 as many men as the other.
The number of men you would put into the SMALLER crew is   8.____
   A. 10   B. 12   C. 14   D. 20

9. It takes 12 asphalt workers, working 6 hours a day, 5 days to complete a certain job. The number of days it will take 10 men, working 8 hours a day, to do the same job, assuming all work at the same rate, is   9.____
   A. 2 1/2   B. 3   C. 4 1/2   D. 6

10. A street is laid to a 3% grade. This means that in 150 ft., the street grade will rise   10.____
    A. 4 1/2 inches
    B. 45 inches
    C. 4 1/2 feet
    D. 45 feet

2 (#3)

11. The sum of the following dimensions, 3 4/8, 4 1/8, 5 1/8, and 6 1/4, is   11.____

    A. 19   B. 19 1/8   C. 19 1/4   D. 19 1/2

12. A worker is paid $9.30 per hour.   12.____
If he works 8 hours each day on Monday, Tuesday, and Wednesday, 3 1/2 hours on Thursday, and 3 hours on Friday, the TOTAL amount due him is

    A. $283.65   B. $289.15   C. $276.20   D. $285.35

13. The price of metal lath is $395.00 per 100 square yards. The cost of 527 square yards of this lath is MOST NEARLY   13.____

    A. $2,076.50   B. $2,079.10   C. $2,081.70   D. $2,084.30

14. The total cost of applying 221 square yards of plaster board is $3,430.   14.____
The cost per square yard is MOST NEARLY

    A. $14.00   B. $14.50   C. $15.00   D. $15.50

15. In a three-coat plaster job, the scratch coat is 1/8 in. thick in front of the lath, the brown coat is 3/16 in. thick, and the finish coat is 1/8 in. thick.   15.____
The TOTAL thickness of this plaster job, measured from the face of the lath, is

    A. 7/16"   B. 1/2"   C. 9/16"   D. 5/8"

16. If an asphalt worker earns $38,070 per year, his wages per month are MOST NEARLY   16.____

    A. $380.70   B. $735.00   C. $3,170.00   D. $3,807.00

17. The sum of 4 1/2 inches, 3 1/4 inches, and 7 1/2 inches is 1 foot _____ inches.   17.____

    A. 3   B. 3 1/4   C. 3 1/2   D. 4

18. The area of a rectangular asphalt patch, 9 ft. 3 in. by 6 ft. 9 in., is _____ square feet.   18.____

    A. 54   B. 54 1/4   C. 54 1/2   D. 62 7/16

19. The number of cubic feet in a cubic yard is   19.____

    A. 3   B. 9   C. 16   D. 27

20. A 450 ft. long street with a grade of 2% will have one end of the street higher than the other end by _____ feet.   20.____

    A. 2   B. 44   C. 9   D. 20

21. If the drive wheel of a roller is 6 ft. in diameter and the tiller wheel is 4 ft. in diameter, whenever the drive wheel makes a complete revolution on a straight pass, the tiller wheel makes _____ revolution(s).   21.____

    A. 1   B. 1 1/4   C. 1 1/2   D. 2

22. A point on the centerline of a street is marked: Station 42 + 51. Another point on the centerline 30 feet from the first is marked Station 42+81.   22.____
A third should be marked Station

    A. 12+51   B. 42+21   C. 45+51   D. 72+51

23. In twenty minutes, a truck moving with a speed of 30 miles an hour will cover a distance   23.____
    of _____ miles.
    A. 3   B. 5   C. 10   D. 30

24. The number of pounds in a ton is   24.____
    A. 500   B. 1,000   C. 2,000   D. 5,000

25. During his summer vacation, a boy earned $45.00 per day and saved 60% of his earn-   25.____
    ings.
    If he worked 45 days, how much did he save during his vacation?
    A. $15.00   B. $18.00   C. $1,215.00   D. $22.50

KEY (CORRECT ANSWERS)

1. D   11. A
2. C   12. A
3. B   13. C
4. B   14. D
5. C   15. A

6. C   16. C
7. A   17. B
8. B   18. D
9. C   19. D
10. C   20. C

21. C
22. B
23. C
24. C
25. C

SOLUTIONS TO PROBLEMS

1. ($4.60)(2 1/4 lbs.) = $10.35

2. 1 gallon = 8 pints, so 20 pints = 20/8 = 2 1/2 gallons

3. $\dfrac{5}{12}+\dfrac{1}{4}=\dfrac{5}{12}+\dfrac{3}{12}=\dfrac{8}{12}=\dfrac{2}{3}$

4. (4')(5 1/2')(18 1/2') = 407 cu.ft. Since 1 cu.yd. = 27 cu.ft., 407 cu.ft. ≈ 15.1 cu.yds.

5. 5/8 = 5 ÷ 8.000 = .625

6. There are (3)(3)(3) = 27 cu.ft. in a cu.yd.

7. (15')(15') = 225 sq.ft. = 25 sq.yds. Then, ($16.20)(25) = $405.00

8. Let 2x = size of smaller crew and 3x = size of larger crew. Then, 2x + 3x = 30. Solving, x = 6. Thus, the smaller crew consists of 12 workers.

9. (12)(6)(5) = 360 worker-days. Then, 360 ÷ [(10)(8)] = 4 1/2 days

10. (.03)(150') = 4 1/2 ft.

11. $3\dfrac{4}{8}+4\dfrac{1}{8}+5\dfrac{1}{8}+6\dfrac{2}{8}=18\dfrac{8}{8}=19$

12. ($9.30)(8+8+8+3 1/2+3) = ($9.30)(30 1/2) = $283.65

13. The cost of 527 sq.yds. = (5.27)($395.00) = $2081.65 ≈ $2081.70

14. $3430 ÷ 221 ≈ $15.50

15. $\dfrac{1}{8}"+\dfrac{3}{16}"+\dfrac{1}{8}"=\dfrac{2}{16}"+\dfrac{3}{16}"+\dfrac{2}{16}"=\dfrac{7}{16}"$

16. $38,070 ÷ 12 = $3172.50 ≈ $3170.00 per month

17. 4 1/2" + 3 1/4" + 7 1/2" = 15 1/4" = 1 ft. 3 1/4 in.

18. 9 ft. 3 in. = 9 1/4 ft., 6 ft. 9 in. = 6 3/4 ft. Area = (9 1/4)(6 3/4) = 62 7/16 sq.ft.

19. A cubic yard = (3)(3)(3) = 27 cubic feet

20. (450')(.02) = 9 ft.

21. 6/4 = 1 1/2 revolutions

22. Station 42 + 51
    30 ft away would be 51 + 30 = 81 OR 51 - 30 = 21
    Station 42 + 81 or 42 + 21 (ANSWER: B)

23. 30 miles in 60 minutes means 10 miles in 20 minutes.

24. There are 2000 pounds in a ton.

25. ($45.00)(.60) = $27.00 savings per day. For 45 days, his savings is (45)($27.00) = $1215.00

EXAMINATION SECTION
TEST 1

DIRECTIONS: Each question or incomplete statement is followed by several suggested answers or completions. Select the one that BEST answers the question or completes the statement. *PRINT THE LETTER OF THE CORRECT ANSWER IN THE SPACE AT THE RIGHT.*

1. Which of the following fractions is the SMALLEST?
   A. 2/3   B. 4/5   C. 5/7   D. 5/11

2. 40% is equivalent to which of the following?
   A. 4/5   B. 4/6   C. 2/5   D. 4/100

3. How many 100's are in 10,000?
   A. 10   B. 100   C. 10,000   D. 100,000

4. $\frac{6}{7} + \frac{11}{12}$ is approximately
   A. 1   B. 2   C. 17   D. 19

5. The time required to heat water to a certain temperature is directly proportional to the volume of water being heated.
   If it takes 12 minutes to heat 1 ½ gallons of water, how many minutes will it take to heat 2 gallons of water?
   A. 12   B. 16   C. 18   D. 24

6. The cost of an item increased by 25%.
   If the original cost was C dollars, identify the expression which gives the new cost of that item.
   A. C + 0.25   B. 1/4 C   C. 25C   D. 1.25C

7. Given the formula PV = nRT, all of the following are true EXCEPT
   A. T = PV/nR   B. P = nRTN   C. V = P/nRT   D. n = PV/RT

8. If a Fahrenheit (F) temperature reading is 104, find its Celsius (C) equivalent, given that C = i(F-32).
   A. 36   B. 40   C. 72   D. 76

9. If 40% of a graduating class plans to go directly to work after graduation, which of the following must be TRUE?
   A. Less than half of the class plans to go directly to work.
   B. Forty members of the class plan to enter the job market.
   C. Most of the class plans to go directly to work.
   D. Six in ten members of the class are expected not to graduate.

10. Given a multiple-choice test item which has 5 choices, what is the probability of guessing the correct answer if you know nothing about the item content?
   A. 5%   B. 10%   C. 20%   D. 25%

10.____

11.

S	T
0	80
5	75
10	65
15	50
20	30
25	5

11.____

Which graph BEST represents the data shown in the above table?

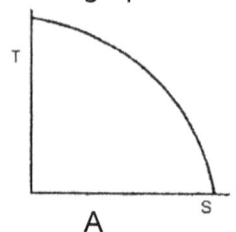 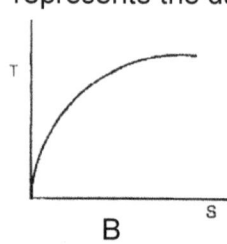 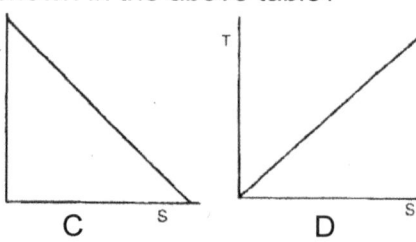

A   B   C   D

12. If 3(x+5y) = 24, find y when x = 3.
   A. 1   B. 3   C. 33/5   D. 7

12.____

13. The payroll of a grocery store for its 23 clerks is $395,421. Which expression below shows the average salary of a clerk?
   A. 395,421 × 23
   B. 23 ÷ 395,421
   C. (395,421 × 23
   D. 395,421 ÷ 23

13.____

14. If 12.8 pounds of coffee cost $50.80, what is the APPROXIMATE price per pound?
   A. $2.00   B. $3.00   C. $4.00   D. $5.00

14.____

15. A road map has a scale where 1 inch corresponds to 150 miles. A distance of 3 3/4 inches on the map corresponds to what actual distance? _____ miles.
   A. 153.75   B. 375   C. 525   D. 562.5

15.____

16. How many square feet of plywood are needed to construct the back and 4 adjacent sides of the box shown at the right?
   A. 63
   B. 90
   C. 96
   D. 126

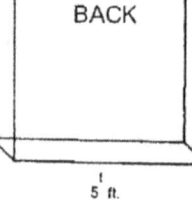

16.____

17. One thirty-pound bag of lawn fertilizer costs $20.00 and will cover 600 square feet of lawn. Terry's lawn is a 96 foot by 75 foot rectangle. How much will it cost Terry to buy enough bags of fertilizer for her lawn?
Which of the following do you NOT need in order to solve this problem? The
A. product of 96 and 75
B. fact that one bag weighs 30 pounds
C. fact that one bag covers 600 square feet
D. fact that one bag costs $20.00

17._____

18. On the graph shown at the right, between which hours was the drop in temperature GREATEST?
A. 11:00 – Noon
B. Noon – 1:00
C. 1:00 – 2:00
D. 2:00 – 3:00

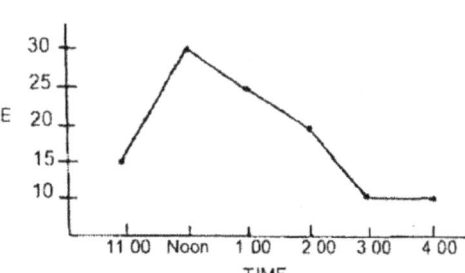

18._____

19. If on a typical railroad track the distance from the center of one railroad tie to the next is 30 inches, approximately how many ties would be needed for one mile of track?
A. 180   B. 2,110   C. 6,340   D. 63,360

19._____

20. Which of the following is MOST likely to be the volume of a wine bottle?
A. 750 milliliters   B. 7 kilograms
C. 7 milligrams   D. 7 liters

20._____

21. What is the reading on the gauge shown at the right?
A. -7
B. -3
C. 1
D. 3

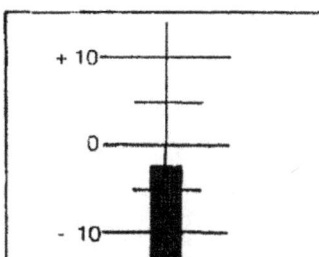

21._____

22. Which statement below disproves the assertion, *All students in Mrs. Marino's 10th grade geometry class are planning to go to college?*
A. Albert is in Mrs. Marino's class, but he is not planning to take mathematics next year.
B. Jorge is not in Mrs. Marino's class, but he is still planning to go to college.
C. Pierre is in Mrs. Marino's class but says he will not be attending school anymore after this year.
D. Crystal is in Mrs. Marino's class and plans to attend Yale University when she graduates.

22._____

23. A store advertisement reads, *Buy not while our prices are low. There will never be a better time to buy.*
    The customer reading this advertisement should assume that
    A. the prices at the store will probably never be lower
    B. right now, this store has the best prices in town
    C. prices are higher at other stores
    D. prices are always lowest at this store

24. Given any positive integer, there is always a positive number B such that A × B is less than 1.
    Which statement below supports this generalization?
    A. 8 × 1/16 = 1/2
    B. 8 × 1/2 = 4
    C. 5/2 × 1/10 = 1/4
    D. 1/2 × 1/2 = 1/2

25. Of the following expressions, which is equivalent to 4C + D = 12E?
    A. C = 4(12E-D)
    B. 4 + D = 12E − C
    C. 4C + 12E = -D
    D. $C = \dfrac{12E-D}{4}$

KEY (CORRECT ANSWERS)

1.	D		11.	A
2.	C		12.	A
3.	B		13.	D
4.	B		14.	C
5.	B		15.	D
6.	D		16.	C
7.	C		17.	B
8.	B		18.	D
9.	A		19.	B
10.	C		20.	A

21. B
22. C
23. A
24. A
25. D

SOLUTIONS TO PROBLEMS

1. Converting to decimals, we get $.\overline{6}$, .8, .714 (approx..), $.\overline{45}$. The smallest is $.\overline{45}$ corresponding to 5/11.

2. 40% = 40/100 = 2/5

3. 10,000 ÷ 100 = 100

4. $\frac{6}{7} + \frac{11}{12}$ = (72+77) ÷ 84 = $\frac{149}{84}$ ≈ 1.77 ≈ 2

5. Let x = required minutes. Then, 12/1 ½ = x^2. This reduces to 1 1/2x = 24. Solving, x = 16.

6. New cost is C + .25C = 1.25C

7. For PV = nRT, V = nRT/P

8. C = 5/9 (104-32) = 5/9(72) = 40

9. Since 40% is less than 50% (or half), we conclude that less than half of the class plans to go to work directly after graduation.

10. The probability of guessing right is 1/5 or 20%

11. Curve A is most accurate since as S increases, we see that T decreases. Note, however, that the relationship is NOT linear. Although S increases in equal amounts, the decrease in T is NOT in equal amounts.

12. 3(3+5y) = 24. This simplifies to 9 + 15y = 24. Solving, y = 1

13. The average salary is $395,421 ÷ 23

14. The price per pound is $50.80 ÷ 12.8 = $3,96875 or approximately $4.

15. Actual distance is (3 3/4)(150) = 562.5 miles.

16. The area of the back = (6)(5) = 30 sq. ft. The combined area of the two vertical sides is (2)(6)(3) = 36 sq. ft. The combined area of the horizontal sides is (2)(5)(3) = 30 sq. ft. Total area = 30 + 36 30 = 96 square feet.

17. Choice B is not relevant to solving the problem since the cost will be [(96)(75)/600][$20] = $240. So, the weight per bag is not needed.

18. For the graph, the largest temperature drop was from 2:00 P.M. to 3:00 P.M. The temperature dropped 20 – 10 = 10 degrees.

19. 1 mile = 5280 feet = 63,360 inches. Then, 63,360 ÷ 30 = 2112 or about 2110 ties are needed.

20. Since 1 liter = 1.06 quarts, 750 milliliters = (750/1000)(1.06) = .795 quarts. This is a reasonable volume for a wine bottle.

21. The reading is -3.

22. Statement C contradicts the given information, since Pierre is in Mrs. Marino's class. Then he should plan to go to college.

23. Since there will never be a better time to buy at this particular store, the customer can assume the current prices will probably never be lower.

24. Statement A illustrates this concept. Note that in general, if n is a positive integer. then $(n)(\frac{1}{n-1}) < 1$

25.

TEST 2

DIRECTIONS: Each question or incomplete statement is followed by several suggested answers or completions. Select the one that BEST answers the question or completes the statement. *PRINT THE LETTER OF THE CORRECT ANSWER IN THE SPACE AT THE RIGHT.*

1. Which of the following lists numbers in INCREASING order? 1._____
   A. 0.4, 0.04, 0.004
   B. 2.71, 3.15, 2.996
   C. 0.7, 0.77, 0.777
   D. 0.06, 0.5, 0.073

2. $\frac{4}{10}+\frac{7}{100}+\frac{5}{1000} =$ 2._____
   A. 4.75   B. 0.475   C. 0.0475   D. 0.00475

3. 700 times what number equals 7? 3._____
   A. 10   B. 0.1   C. 0.01   D. 0.001

4. 943-251 is approximately 4._____
   A. 600   B. 650   C. 700   D. 1200

5. The time needed to set up a complicated piece of machinery is inversely proportional to the number of years' experience of the worker. 5._____
   If a worker with 10 years' experience needs 6 hours to do the job, how long will it take a worker with 15 years' experience?
   A. 4   B. 5   C. 9   D. 25

6. Let W represent the number of waiters and D, the number of diners in a particular restaurant. 6._____
   Identify the expression which represents the statement: There are 10 times as many diners as waiters.
   A. 10W = D   B. 10D = W   C. 10D + 10W   D. 10 = D + W

7. Which of the following is equivalent to the formula F = XC + Y? 7._____
   A. F − C = X + Y
   B. Y = F + XC
   C. $C = \frac{FY}{X}$
   D. $C = \frac{FX}{Y}$

8. Given the formula A = BC/D, if A = 12, B = 6, and D = 3, what is the value of C? 8._____
   A. 2/3   B. 6   C. 18   D. 24

9. 5 is to 7 as X is to 35. X = 9._____
   A. 7   B. 12   C. 24   D. 49

10. Kramer Middle School has 5 seventh grade mathematics teachers: two of the math teachers are women and three are men. 10._____
    If you are assigned a teacher at random, what is the probability of getting a female teacher?
    A. 0.2   B. 0.4   C. 0.6   D. 0.8

11. Which statement BEST describes the graph shown at the right?
    Temperature
    A. and time decrease at the same rate
    B. and time increase at the same rate
    C. increases over time
    D. decreases over time

12. If 3x + 4 = 22y, find y when x = 2.
    A. 0   B. 3   C. 4 1/2   D. 5

13. A car goes 243 miles on 8.7 gallons of gas.
    Which numeric expression should be used to determine the car's miles per gallon?
    A. 243 × 87   B. 8.7 ÷ 243   C. 243 ÷ 8.7   D. 243 − 8.7

14. What is the average cost per book if you buy six books at $4.00 each and four books at $5.00 each?
    A. $4.40   B. $4.50   C. $4.60   D. $5.40

15. A publisher's sale offers a 15% discount to anyone buying more than 100 workbooks.
    What will be the discount on 200 workbooks selling at $2.25 each?
    A. $15.00   B. $30.00   C. $33.75   D. $67.50

16. A road crew erects 125 meters of fencing in one workday.
    How many workdays are required to erect a kilometer of fencing?
    A. 0.8   B. 8   C. 80   D. 800

17. Last month Kim made several telephone calls to New York City totaling 45 minutes in all.
    What does Kim need in order to calculate the average duration of her New York City calls?
    The
    A. total number of calls she made to New York City
    B. cost per minute of a call to New York City
    C. total cost of her telephone bill last month
    D. days of the week on which the calls are made

18.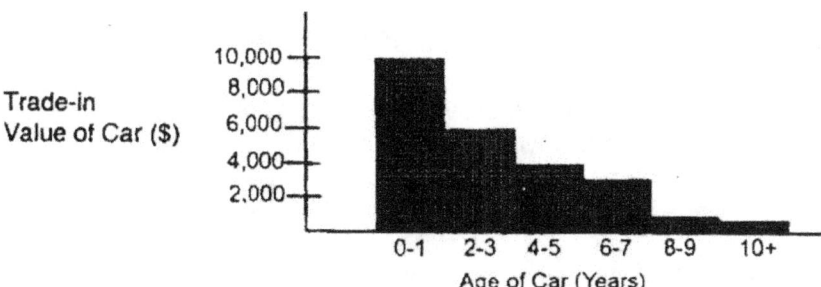

The above chart relates a car's age to its trade-in value.
Based on the chart, which of the following is TRUE?
- A. A 4- to 5-year old car has a trade-in value of about $2,000
- B. The trade-in vale of an 8- to 9-year old car is about 1/3 that of a 2- to 3-year old car.
- C. A 6- to 7-year old car has no trade-in value.
- D. A 4- to 5-year old car's trade-in value is about $2,000 less than that of a 2- to 3-year old car.

18.____

19. Which of the following expressions could be used to determine how many seconds are in a 24-hour day?
- A. 60 × 60 × 24
- B. 60 × 12 × 24
- C. 60 × 2 × 24
- D. 60 × 24

19.____

20. For measuring milk, we could use each of the following EXCEPT
- A. liters
- B. kilograms
- C. millimeters
- D. cubic centimeters

20.____

21. What is the reading on the gauge shown at the right?
- A. 51
- B. 60
- C. 62.5
- D. 70

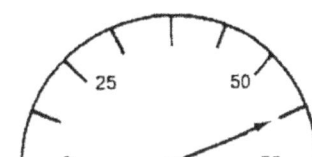

21.____

22. Bill is taller than Yvonne. Yvonne is shorter than Sue. Sue is 5' tall.
Which of the following conclusions must be TRUE?
- A. Bill is taller than Sue.
- B. Yvonne is taller than 5'4".
- C. Sue is taller than Bill.
- D. Yvonne is the shortest.

22.____

23. The Bass family traveled 268 miles during the first day of their vacation and another 300 miles on the next day. Maria Bass said they were 568 miles from home.
Which of the following facts did Maria assume?
- A. They traveled faster on the first day and slower on the second.
- B. If she plotted the vacation route on a map, it would be a straight line.
- C. Their car used more gasoline on the second day.
- D. They traveled faster on the second day than they did on the first day.

23.____

24. *The word LEFT in a mathematics problem indicate that it is a subtraction problem.*
Which of the following mathematics problems prove this statement FALSE?
   A. I want to put 150 bottles into cartons which hold 8 bottles each. After I completely fill as many cartons as I can, how many bottles will be left?
   B. Sarah has 5 books but gave one to John. How many books did Sarah have left?
   C. Carlos had $4.25 but spent $3.75. How much did he have left?
   D. We had 38 models in stock but after yesterday's sale, only 12 are left. How many did we sell?

25. Let Q represent the number of miles Dave can jog in 15 minutes.
Identify the expression which represents the number of miles Dave can jog between 3:00 P.M. and 4:45 P.M.
   A. 1 3/4 Q   B. 7Q   C. 15 × 1 3/4xQ   D. Q/7

KEY (CORRECT ANSWERS)

1.	C	11.	D
2.	B	12.	D
3.	C	13.	C
4.	C	14.	A
5.	A	15.	D
6.	A	16.	B
7.	C	17.	A
8.	B	18.	D
9.	C	19.	A
10.	B	20.	C

21. C
22. D
23. B
24. A
25. B

5 (#2)

SOLUTIONS TO PROBLEMS

1. Choice C is in ascending order since .y < .77 < .777

2. Rewrite in decimal form: .4 + .07 + .005 = .475

3. Let x = missing number. Then, 700x = 7. Solving, x = 7/700 = .01

4. 943 − 251 = 692 ≈ 700

5. Let x = hours needed. Then, 10/15 = x/6. Solving, x = 4

6. The number of diners (D) is 10 times as many waiters (10W). So, D = 10W, or 10W = D

7. Given F = XC + Y, subtract Y from each side to get F − Y = XC. Finally, dividing by X, we get (F-Y)/X = C

8. 12 = 6C/3. Then, 12 = 2C, so C = 6

9. 5/7 = x/35. Then, 7x = 175, so x = 25

10. Probability of a female teacher = 2/5 = .4

11. Statement D is best, since as time increases, the temperature decreases.

12. (3)(2) + 4 = 2y. Then, 10 = 2y, so y = 5.

13. Miles per gallon = 243/8.7

14. Total purchase is (6)($4) + (4)($5) = $44. The average cost per book is $44 ÷ 10 = $4.40

15. (220)($2.25) = $450. The discount is (.15))($450) = $67.50

16. The number of workdays is 1000 ÷ 125 = 8

17. Choice A is correct because the average duration of the phone calls = total time ÷ total number of calls.

18. Statement D is correct since a 4-5 year old car's value is $4,000, whereas a 2-3 year-old car's value is $6000.

19. 60 seconds = 1 minute and 60 minutes = 1 hour. Thus, 24 hours = (24)(60)(60) or (60)(60)(24) seconds.

20. We can't use millimeters in measuring milk since millimeters is a linear measurement.

21. The reading shows the average of 50 and 75 = 62.5

22. Since Yvonne is shorter than both Bill and Sue, Yvonne is the shortest.

23. Statement B is assumed correct since 568 = 269 + 300 could only be true if the mileage traveled represents a straight line.

24. To find the number of bottles left, we look only for the remainder when 150 is divided b 8 (which happens to be 6).

25. 3:00 P.M. to 4:45 P.M. = 1 hour and 45 minutes = 105 minutes
Let Q = 15 minutes
105 / 15 = 7
7(15) = 105 = 7Q

EXAMINATION SECTION
TEST 1

DIRECTIONS: Each question or incomplete statement is followed by several suggested answers or completions. Select the one that BEST answers the question or completes the statement. *PRINT THE LETTER OF THE CORRECT ANSWER IN THE SPACE AT THE RIGHT.*

1. What is the safe working pressure, in pounds, of a boiler with a 5/8 inch plate, 60,000 lb. tensile strength, 60 inch diameter and triple riveted joints, using a factor of safety of 5?

   (Use the formula: Safe working pressure $= \frac{2XSXTXE}{FXT}$)

   A. 115 B. 185.5
   C. 217.5 D. None of the above

2. What is the mechanical efficiency of an engine which delivers 200 brake H.P. while showing 250 indicated H.P.?

   (Use the formula: Mechanical efficiency $= \frac{\text{Brake H.P.}}{\text{Indicated H.P.}}$)

   A. 80% B. 90% C. 95% D. 100%

3. A pump delivers 500 cubic feet of water per minute and the pump displacement is 560 cubic feet. What is the slip?

   (Use the formula: Slip $= \frac{\text{Displacement - Volumn}}{\text{Displacement}}$)

   A. 10.7% B. 15.5% C. 18.7% D. 21.3%

4. A boiler is operating under 120 psi absolute pressure with feedwater at 160°F. The factor of evaporation is 1.063.5/970.4 = 1.097.
   If the total evaporation is 8,760 lb/hr., what boiler horsepower is the boiler developing?
   (Use the formula:

   Boiler H.P. $= \frac{\text{Total Evaporation x Factor of Evaporation}}{34.5}$)

   A. 300 B. 278 C. 236 D. 212

5. If an ammonia system was working at 15 lb. gage suction pressure and the temperature of liquid ammonia entering the evaporator through the expansion valve was 90°F., how many BTU per lb. would be available for useful work, assuming that the total heat of 1 lb. of ammonia at
   15 lb. gage pressure is 611.4 BTU and the heat of the liquid at 90°F. is 143.5 BTU?

   A. 376.5 B. 422.7 C. 467.9 D. 494.8

6. The sine of 120° is the same as the sine of

   A. 45°
   B. 60°
   C. 45° but with a negative sign
   D. 60° but with a negative sign

7. In a circular curve of radius R and central angle I, the distance is used to locate the

   A. point of curvature
   B. point of intersection or vertex
   C. center of the curve from the vertex
   D. midpoint of the chord of the circular curve

8. The formula for the area of a triangle is

   A. 1/2ab sin A   B. 1/2bc sin A   C. 1/2ac cos A   D. 1/2ab cosA

9. The logarithm of 7 is approximately 0.845.
   The logarithm of $(0.007)^{1/4}$ is APPROXIMATELY

   A. 9.343-10   B. 9.567-10   C. 9.461-10   D. 9.561-10

10. The center of gravity of a triangle is located at the intersection of the

    A. angle bisectors
    B. medians
    C. perpendicular bisectors of the sides
    D. radians

11. The distance between two stations was measured six times, and the average distance found to be 346.215 ft.
    If one measurement of 351.205 ft. is deleted from the data as being inconsistent with the other measurements, then the average of the remaining five measurements is, in feet,

    A. 345.217   B. 345.221   C. 345.227   D. 345.235

12. A map of an area 380 ft. x 740 ft. is to be plotted on a sheet of drawing paper.
    The SMALLEST sheet of paper required to plot this map to a scale of 1" = 50', leaving a one-inch margin all around, is, in inches,

    A. 8 1/2 x 11   B. 10 x 17   C. 12 x 17   D. 10 x 15

13. On a topographic map, widely spaced contour lines indicate

    A. a gentle slope   B. a steep slope
    C. an overhanging cliff   D. the bank of a stream

14. The scale to which a map is drawn is 1" = 800'.
    IOf the following, the MOST common method by which this scale would be indicated on the map is

    A. 1/800   B. 1" - 9600"
    C. 8.0" = one mile   D. 1/9600

15. The angle formed between one line and the prolongation of the preceding line in a closed traverse is known as _____ angle.   15._____

    A. split
    B. obtuse
    C. direction
    D. deflection

16. When laying out a horizontal circular curve, the deflection angle for a 100 ft. chord is equal to _____ of curvature.   16._____

    A. one-quarter of the degree
    B. one-half of the degree
    C. three-quarters of the degree
    D. the degree

17. For a given intersection angle, tables of the functions of a one degree curve show the tangent distance to be 1062.0 ft.   17._____

    For the same intersection angle and a curvature of 4°, the tangent distance is, in feet, MOST NEARLY

    A. 265.5   B. 437.9   C. 649.3   D. 1153.4

18. Assume that a certain pumping station has three pumps A, B, and C. A can pump 1,000 gallons in 6 minutes, B can pump 1,000 gallons in 3 minutes, and C can pump 1,000 gallons in 2 minutes.   18._____
    The time required for all three pumps working at the same time to pump 1,000 gallons is MOST NEARLY _____. minute(s).

    A. 2   B. 1   C. 14 1/2   D. 1/2

19. Of the following, the equation of a line tangent to the graph of $x^2 + y^2 = 81$ is   19._____

    A. $x = 9$ B. $x + y = 9$ C. $x = 9y$ D. $x = -9y$

20. Of the following, the equation whose roots are -3 and 2 is   20._____

    A. $2x^2 + 3x - 6 = 0$
    B. $x^2 + x - 6 = 0$
    C. $x^2 - x + 6 = 0$
    D. $x^2 + 6 = 0$

21. The sum of 10 1/2, 8 3/4, 51/2, and 2 1/4 is   21._____

    A. 23   B. 25   C. 26   D. 27

22. A water tank measures 50 feet long, 16 feet wide, and 12 feet high. Assume that water weighs 60 pounds per cubic foot and that one gallon of water weighs 8 pounds. The number of gallons the tank can hold when it is half full is   22._____

    A. 21,500   B. 28,375   C. 33,410   D. 36,000

23. Assuming 70 gallons of oil cost $84.00, then 110 gallons of oil at the same rate will cost   23._____

    A. $132.00   B. $168.00   C. $192.00   D. $304.00

24. Three 75-gallon per hour mechanical pressure type oil burners operating together are to burn 150,000 gallons of No. 6 fuel oil.   24._____
    The number of hours they would take to burn this amount of oil is MOST NEARLY

    A. 665   B. 760   C. 870   D. 1210

25. A supplier quotes a list price of $68.00 less discounts of 25 and 20 percent for a replacement part. The actual cost of this item is MOST NEARLY   25._____

    A. $31   B. $34   C. $37   D. $41

KEY (CORRECT ANSWERS)

1.	D	11.	A
2.	A	12.	B
3.	A	13.	A
4.	B	14.	D
5.	C	15.	D
6.	B	16.	B
7.	C	17.	A
8.	B	18.	B
9.	C	19.	A
10.	B	20.	B

21. D
22. D
23. A
24. A
25. D

SOLUTIONS TO PROBLEMS

1. 1, 16

2. Mechanical efficiency = 200/250 = 80%

3. Slip = (560 - 500) ÷ 560 = 10.7%

4. Boiler horsepower = (8760)(1.097) ÷ 34.5 ≈ 278

5. BTU = 611.4 - 143.5 = 467.9

6. Sin 120° = sin 60° ≈ .866

7. The distance from the center of a circular curve of radius R from the vertex (central $\angle = I$) is $R(\frac{1}{\cos 1/2 I} - 1)$ = Rtan 1/2tan 1/4I

8. Area of a triangle = (1/2)(any 2 sides)(sine of the angle between these sides) = 1/2bc sin A. Other possibilities are 1/2ab sin C and 1/2ac sin B.

9. $Log(.007)^{\frac{1}{4}}$ = 1/4Log(7×10^{-3}) = 1/4(Log 7 - 3) ≈ 1/4(.845 - 3) ≈ .539 = 9.461 - 10

10. The medians of a triangle intersect at the center of gravity.

11. (6)(346.215) = 2077.29. Then, (2077.29 - 351.205) 5 = 345.217 ft.

12. 380 ft. is represented by 380/50 = 7.6" and 740 ft. is represented by 740/50 = 14.8". Allowing for a border of 1" on all 4 sides requires a sheet of paper at least 10" x 17"

13. On a topographic map, widely spaced contour lines indicate a gentle slope, while contour lines drawn close together indicate a steep slope.

14. $\frac{1"}{800'} = \frac{1"}{(800)(12)"} = \frac{1}{9600}$

15. A deflection angle is formed between a line and the extension of another line already extant in a closed traverse.

16. One-half of the degree of curvature, by empirical knowledge.

17. The tangent distances are inversely proportional to the curvature angles. Let x = tangent distance. Then, 1062/x = 4/1
    Solving, x = 265.5 ft.

18. Let x = number of minutes when all 3 pumps are working. Then, $1/6x + 1/3x + 1/2x = 1$. Simplifying, $x+2x+3x=6$. Solving, $x = 1$

19. The graph of $x^2 + y^2 = 81$ is a circle with center at (0, 0) and a radius of 9. The line $x = 9$ is vertical and tangent to this circle at (9,0).

20. Given roots -3 and 2, the equation becomes $(x+3)(x-2) = 0$. This is equivalent to $x^2 + x - 6 = 0$

21. 10 1/2 + 8 3/4 + 5 1/2 + 2 1/4 = 25 8/4 = 27

22. Total water weight = (60)(50)(16)(12) = 576,000 pounds.
Then, 288,000 pounds is the weight when the tank is half full. Finally, 288,000 ÷ 8 = 36,000 gallons

23. Let x = cost. Then, $\frac{70}{110} = \frac{\$84.00}{x}$. Solving, x = $132.00

24. 150,000 ÷ [(3)(75)] = 666 2/3 hours, closest to 665 hours.

25. Actual cost = ($68.00)(.75)(.80) = $40.80 ≈ $41

TEST 2

DIRECTIONS: Each question or incomplete statement is followed by several suggested answers or completions. Select the one that BEST answers the question or completes the statement. *PRINT THE LETTER OF THE CORRECT ANSWER IN THE SPACE AT THE RIGHT.*

1. A street has a grade of 1 1/2%.
   The distance the street rises in 1 1/2 miles is MOST NEARLY, in feet,   1.____

   A. 79.20   B. 98.75   C. 103.50   D. 118.80

2. The signs of the sine, cosine, and tangent of an angle are all positive in Quadrant   2.____

   A. I   B. II   C. III   D. IV

3. The sum of three interior angles of a four-sided parcel of land add up to 115°.
   The fourth interior angle, in degrees, is   3.____

   A. 25   B. 75   C. 245   D. 295

4. A circular tank is 12 feet in diameter and 9 feet high. The depth of water in the tank is 1/3 from the top. There are 7 1/2 gallons in a cubic foot.
   The number of gallons of water in the tank is MOST NEARLY   4.____

   A. 4,820   B. 5,090   C. 5,320   D. 5,570

5. If log of 2 = 0.3010 and log of 3 = 0.4772, then the log of 36 equals   5.____

   A. 0.7782   B. 1.0792   C. 1.2554   D. 1.5564

6. If there are 43,560 square feet in an acre, the number of acres in a tract 2 miles long by 3.2 miles wide is MOST NEARLY   6.____

   A. 3,750   B. 4,100   C. 4,350   D. 4,600

7. A foundation for a building consists of 9 concrete footings 8 ft. by 6 ft. by 18 inches deep.
   The total number of cubic yards of concrete in the footings is   7.____

   A. 12   B. 24   C. 36   D. 72

8. Two applications at 0.4 gallons per square yard of bituminous material on a half mile of road 18 feet wide would require MOST NEARLY _____ gallons.   8.____

   A. 425   B. 3,875   C. 4,225   D. 38,000

9. Rock excavation is to be paid for at a unit price of $75/cubic yard.
   Of the following, the cost of rock between Sta. 3+35 and Sta. 8+65 for a width of 45 feet and a depth of five feet is MOST NEARLY   9.____

   A. $225,000   B. $330,000   C. $660,000   D. $990,000

10. Three 40-foot long piles are driven so that their top elevations are 79.6', 81.7', and 80.2' before being cut off at elevation 75.5'.
    If the contract unit price is $13.50 per foot in place, then the payment to the contractor is MOST NEARLY   10.____

    A. $1,215.00   B. $1,417.50   C. $1,620.00   D. $1,800.00

11. In the sketch shown at the right, the length of X is
    A. 8.0
    B. 9.0
    C. 9.5
    D. 10.0

12. In Circle O, inscribed angle ABC and central angle AOC have the same intercepted arc AC in common.
    Of the following relationships between angle AOC and angle ABC, the one which is TRUE is that

    A. angle ABC equals angle AOC
    B. angle AOC equals one-half angle ABC
    C. angle ABC equals one-half angle AOC
    D. nothing can be said about their relative sizes solely on the basis of the information given

13. The scale of a drawing is 1/8" = 1'0". A rectangle on the drawing actually measures 7 1/8" x 6 1/4".
    This represents the true area in square feet of MOST NEARLY

    A. 72   B. 144   C. 1,375   D. 2,850

14. The length of AB is, in feet, MOST NEARLY
    A. 130
    B. 135
    C. 140
    D. 145

15. An inspector estimated that a paving job would require 20 cubic yards of concrete. The volume of the concrete actually used was 27.5 cubic yards.
    The percentage of error in the inspector's estimate is MOST NEARLY

    A. 40   B. 38   C. 36   D. 34

16. For a 20 foot ladder, the base should extend back from the face of the wall APPROXIMATELY _____ feet.

    A. 3   B. 5   C. 7   D. 10

17. $\frac{\pi}{2}$ radian is equivalent to, in degrees,

    A. 22 1/2   B. 45   C. 90   D. 180

18. The $\sqrt{690}$ is MOST NEARLY

    A. 26.25   B. 26.27   C. 26.29   D. 26.30

19. The line y = 2x + 8 intersects the x axis at 19._____
    A. -4   B. +4   C. -2   D. +8

20. If the radius of the circle shown at the right is 5", the area of 20._____
    the shaded area, in square inches, is MOST NEARLY
    A. 5.1
    B. 7.1
    C. 7.6
    D. 8.1

21. A cone has a base whose area is A and its altitude is h. The volume of this cone is 21._____
    A. Ah   B. 1/2Ah   C. 1/3Ah   D. 1/4Ah

22. If Y = X^{2x}, the value of Y for X = 3 is 22._____
    A. 27   B. 81   C. 243   D. 729

23. The equation 3x^3 - 5x^2 - 15x - 1 = y will cross the x axis for values of x between x = 23._____
    _____ and x = _____.
    A. 0; 1   B. 1; 2   C. 2; 3   D. 3; 4

24. The shape of the surface created by a plane cut- 24._____
    ting the right cone as shown at the right would be
    a(n)
    A. parabola
    B. hyperbola
    C. ellipse
    D. circle

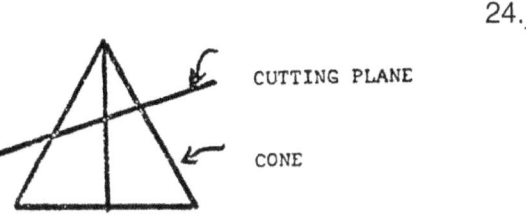

25. The area of the shaded part of the circle shown at the right 25._____
    is MOST NEARLY
    A. 6.1
    B. 7.1
    C. 8.1
    D. 9.1

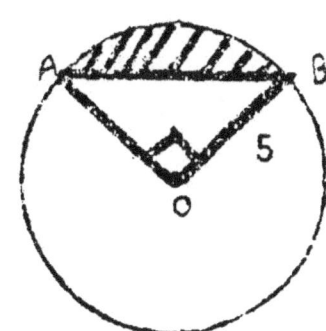

KEY (CORRECT ANSWERS)

1. D
2. A
3. C
4. B
5. D

6. B
7. B
8. C
9. B
10. B

11. D
12. C
13. D
14. B
15. B

16. B
17. C
18. B
19. A
20. A

21. C
22. D
23. D
24. C
25. B

SOLUTIONS TO PROBLEMS

1. Let x = required distance. Then, x/7920 = .015 . So, x = 118.80 ft.
   Note: 1 1/2 mi. = (1 1/2)(5280) = 7920 ft.

2. In Quadrant I, sine, cosine, tangent of any angle is positive.

3. The 4th angle = $360°$ - $115°$ = $245°$

4. Volume of water = (2/3) (π) (6^2) (9) = 216 π cu.ft. Then, (7.5)(216 π) $\approx$ 5091 gallons, closest to 5090 gallons.

5. Log 36 = Log($2^2 \cdot 3^2$) = 2Log 2 + 2Log 3 = 2(.3010) + 2(.4772) = 1.5564

6. (2)(3.2) = 6.4 sq.miles = (6.4)(5280)(5280) = 178,421,760 sq.ft.
   Then, 178,421,760 $\div$ 43,560 = 4096, closest to 4100 acres.

7. (9)(8')(6')(1 1/2') = 648 cu.ft. = 648/27 = 24 cu.yds.

8. (1/2 mi.)(18 ft.) = (880 yds.) (6 yds.) = 5280 sq.yds. Two applications requires (5280)(.4)(2) = 4224, closest to 4225 gallons.

9. 865 - 335 = 530. Then, (530)(45)(5) = 119,250 cu.ft. = 4416 2/3 cu.yds. Finally, ($75) (4416 2/3) = $331,250, which is closest to $330,000.

10. (75.5' - 40')(3) = 106.5'. Then, (106.5)($13.50) = $1437.75, which is closest to $1417.50

11. $\frac{EC}{EB} = \frac{GC}{AB}$, so $\frac{12}{18} = \frac{GC}{12}$ = 8. Now, $(BC)^2 + (GC)^2 = (GB)^2$, so 36 + 64 = $(GB)^2$. Solving, GB = 10

12. $\angle ADC$ = intercept arc in degrees and $\angle ABC$ =1/2 times the intercepted arc. Thus, <ABC = (1/2)($\angle ADC$)

13. 7 1/8" x 6 1/4" is actually (57)(50) = 2850 sq.ft.

14. Draw $\overline{AC}//\overline{ED}$, so that $\triangle$ ACB has a right angle at C.
    BC = 60' - 10' = 50', AC = ED = 125'. Now, $125^2 + 50^2 = (AB)^2$. Solving, AB = $\sqrt{18,125} \approx 135$ ft.

15. (27.5 - 20) $\div$ 20 = 37 1/2% $\approx$ 38%

16. For safety, the angle of elevation between the ladder and the ground should be $75°$. Let x = required distance. Then,
    cos $75°$ = x/20 Solving, x $\approx$ 5 ft.

17. $\frac{\pi}{2}$ radians $= (\frac{\pi}{2}) \frac{180}{\pi} = 90°$

18. $\sqrt{690} \approx 26.27$

19. Let y = 0 in the equation y = 2x + 8. Then, 0 = 2x + 8, so x = -4

20. Area of entire circle = $(\pi)(5^2)$ = 25π. If the central angle is 80°, the area of the sector bounded by A, O, B = $(25\pi)(80/360)$ = $5.\overline{5}\pi$. Area of $\triangle AOB$ = [(1/2)(AO)(OB) (sin 80°)] = (1/2)(5)(5)(sin 80°) $\approx$ 12.31. Finally, the shaded area = 5.5π - 12.31 $\approx$ 5.14 $\approx$ 5.1 sq.in.

21. V = 1/3 Ah for the volume of a cone with base area of A and a height of h.

22. $Y = 3^{2 \cdot 3} = 3^6 = 729$

23. Given $y = 3x^3 - 5x^2 - 15x - 1$, the values of y for x = 0, 1, 2, 3, and 4 are: -1, -18, -12, -10, and 51, respectively. Since the graph must cross the x-axis whenever the y value changes sign, this will take place between x = 3 and x = 4. (Incidentally, the graph also crosses the x-axis at approximately x = -.1 and x = -1.5)

24. Whenever a plane cuts a right circular cone at an acute angle, the surface created is an ellipse.

25. Area of sector AOB = $(1/4)(\pi)(25)$ = 6.25π. Area of $\triangle ADB$ = (1/2)(5)(5) = 12.5. Finally, shaded area = 6.25π - 12.5 $\approx$ 7.1

TEST 3

DIRECTIONS: Each question or incomplete statement is followed by several suggested answers or completions. Select the one that BEST answers the question or completes the statement. *PRINT THE LETTER OF THE CORRECT ANSWER IN THE SPACE AT THE RIGHT.*

1. The equation $\frac{x^2}{a^2} - \frac{y^2}{b^2} = 1$ is the formula for a(n)

   A. cantenary   B. ellipse   C. hyperbola   D. cycloid

2. A pile plan shows fifteen concrete-filled 18" inside diameter steel piles each 35 feet long. If the cost of concrete in place is $120 a cubic yard, then the total cost of the concrete in the piles is MOST NEARLY

   A. $3,750   B. $4,140   C. $4,350   D. $4,500

3. The coverage of a gallon of paint is 400 square feet. The MINIMUM number of gallons required to paint four walls of four rooms each 18 feet by 16 feet by 8 feet high is

   A. 4   B. 5   C. 6   D. 7

4. If there are 22 bricks in a square foot of a 12 inch thick wall, then the number of bricks in a 6 foot wall around a parcel of land 32 feet by 110 feet is MOST NEARLY

   A. 37,000   B. 37,250   C. 37,500   D. 37,750

5. The number of significant figures in 0.0000556 is

   A. 2   B. 3   C. 4   D. 5

6.

	30°	60°
sin	.500	.867
cos	.867	.500
tan	.577	1.732

   In the sketch shown above, the number of feet in the perimeter is MOST NEARLY

   A. 100   B. 105   C. 115   D. 122

7. If the central angle of a circle is 1/3 of a radian, then the number of degrees in the central angle is MOST NEARLY

   A. 6   B. 9.5   C. 12   D. 19

8. The $\sqrt{465}$ is MOST NEARLY

   A. 20.56   B. 21.13   C. 21.34   D. 21.56

9. 90° is MOST NEARLY equal to _____ radians.

   A. 0.5   B. 1.5   C. 2.5   D. 3.5

10. When .68 feet is converted to inches, the result is MOST NEARLY

    A. 7 7/8"   B. 8"   C. 8 1/8"   D. 8 1/4"

11. A 100' guy wire, stretched tight from the top of a vertical pole, makes a 60° angle with the level ground.
The height of this pole, in feet, is MOST NEARLY (sin 60° = .867; cos 60° = .500)

    A. 50   B. 87   C. 100   D. 200

12. The area of a 120° sector of a circle whose radius is 3" is MOST NEARLY _____ square inches.

    A. 7.9   B. 9.42   C. 11.3   D. 12.5

13. The product $\dfrac{6xy}{(x^2-4)} \cdot \dfrac{5x-10}{3xy}$ is equal to

    A. $\dfrac{2xy}{x^2-10}$ B. $\dfrac{30x^2}{x^2y}$ C. $\dfrac{10}{x+2}$ D. $\dfrac{18x^3y}{x+10}$

14. The $\sin^2 x$ is equal to

    A. $1 - 2\cos^2 x$ B. $1 + 2\cos^2 x$
    C. $1 + \cos^2 x$ D. $1 - \cos^2 x$

15. The volume of a cylinder with a radius r and height h is

    A. $\pi r^2 h$ B. $2\pi rh$ C. $2\pi r^2 h$ D. $4\pi r^2 h$

16. The expression reduces to

    A. $\sqrt{7}$ B. $3\sqrt{7}$ C. $\sqrt{21}$ D. $-\sqrt{35}$

17. If $\sin 2x = 1$, then x is

    A. 30°   B. 45°   C. 60°   D. 75°

18. The expression $\dfrac{x^2 y^2}{y} - \dfrac{x^2}{x^4} + y^0$ reduces to

    A. $\dfrac{xy}{x^4}$ B. $\dfrac{y^2}{y-x^4}$ C. $\dfrac{y-1}{x^2}+1$ D. $\dfrac{y-1}{x^2+y}$

19. If the coordinates of E and F in the X-Y plane are (1,-1) and (4,3), respectively, then the length of line E - F is

    A. 4   B. 5   C. 6   D. 7

20. If there are 43,560 square feet in an acre and 640 acres in a square mile, then the number of acres in a tract of land 2640 feet by 7920 feet is MOST NEARLY

    A. 640   B. 480   C. 360   D. 10

21. Point B is 3 miles north and 4 miles east of point A. A person traveling in a straight line from A to B and back again to A would travel a distance EQUAL to _____ miles.

    A. 14   B. 12   C. 10   D. 5

22. The flow from a wide open fire hydrant is 300 gallons per minute. When the hydrant is equipped with a spray nozzle, the flow is reduced to 20 gallons per minute. Over a period of 8 hours, the quantity of water saved by installing a spray nozzle is MOST NEARLY _____ gallons.

    A. 146,200   B. 134,400   C. 56,500   D. 2,400

23. A rectangular building is 100 feet long and 40 feet wide. Waterproofing is to be applied to the exterior of the 10-foot high basement walls at the rate of 2.5 gallons per 100 square feet of wall.
    The number of gallons of waterproofing requires is MOST NEARLY

    A. 70   B. 60   C. 28   D. 10

24. An angle is measured 4 times, and the total of the four readings is 186° 41'22". The angle is MOST NEARLY

    A. 47° 10'12.0"
    C. 46° 32'17.6"
    B. 46° 40'20.5"
    D. 45° 30'15.4"

25. A square tract of land contains 57,600 square feet. The length of a fence needed to enclose the entire property is MOST NEARLY _____ feet.

    A. 960   B. 752   C. 480   D. 300

KEY (CORRECT ANSWERS)

1.	C	11.	B
2.	B	12.	B
3.	C	13.	C
4.	C	14.	D
5.	B	15.	A
6.	D	16.	A
7.	D	17.	B
8.	D	18.	C
9.	B	19.	B
10.	C	20.	B

21. C
22. B
23. A
24. B
25. A

___

SOLUTIONS TO PROBLEMS

1. $\frac{x^2}{a^2} - \frac{y^2}{b^2} = 1$ represents a hyperbola with vertices at $(\pm a, 0)$ and foci at $(\pm c, 0)$, where $c^2 = a^2 + b^2$

2. Total volume (in cu.ft.) of all 15 piles = $(15)(\pi)(.75)(.75)(35) = 295.3125\pi \approx 927.75$.
   Converting to cu.yds., $927.75 \div 27 \approx 34.36$.
   Finally, $(34.36)(\$120) \approx \$4123$, closest to $\$4140$

3. 544 sq.ft. x 4 rooms = 2176 ÷ 400 = 5.4 gallons = 6 gallons

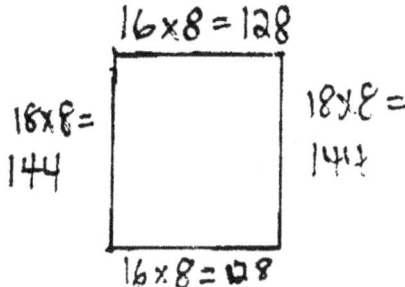

4. Total wall area = $(2)(6)(32) + (2)(6)(110) = 1704$ sq.ft. Then, $(1704)(22) = 37,488$ bricks, closest to 37,500 bricks.

5. .0000556 has 3 significant (non-zero) figures.

6. AD = $(15)/(\sin 60°) \approx 17$ ft., BC = $(15)/(\sin 30°) = 30$ ft., DE = $15/(\tan 60°) \approx 9$ ft., and FC = $15/(\tan 30°)$ 26 ft.
   Thus, DC $\approx 9 + 20 + 26 = 55$ ft. Perimeter of ABCD = $20 + 30 + 55 + 17 = 122$ ft.

7. 1/3 radian = $(1/3)\frac{180}{\pi} = \frac{60}{\pi} \sim 19$ degrees

8. $\sqrt{465} \approx 21.56$

9. $90° = 1/2\pi$ radians ≈ 1.57 radians, closest to 1.5 radians

10. .68 ft. = $(.68)(12) = 8.16$ in., closest to 8 1/8 in.

11. Let x = height of pole. Then, $\sin 60° = x/100$ This becomes $.867 = x/100$. Solving, $x \approx 87$ ft.

12. Area of 120° sector = (1/3)(area of circle) = $(1/3)(\pi)(3^2)$ 9.42 sq.in.

13. $\dfrac{6xy}{(x-2)(x+2)} \cdot \dfrac{5(x-2)}{3xy} = \dfrac{10}{(x-2)}$

14. $\sin^2 x = 1 - \cos^2 x$ always

15. $V = \pi r^2 h$ is the volume of a cylinder with radius = r and height = h

16. $\sqrt{28} - \sqrt{7} = \sqrt{4 \cdot 7} - \sqrt{7} = 2\sqrt{7} - \sqrt{7} = \sqrt{7}$

17. If $\sin 2x = 1$, then $2x = 90°$, so $x = 45°$

18. $\dfrac{x^{-2}y^2}{y} \cdot \dfrac{x^2}{x^4} + y^0 = \dfrac{y}{x^2} \cdot \dfrac{1}{x^2} + 1 = \dfrac{y-1}{x^2} + 1$

19. $EF = \sqrt{(1-4)^2 + (-1-3)^2} = \sqrt{9+16} = 5$

20. (2640')(7920') = 20,908,800 sq.ft. Then, 20,908,800 ÷ 43,560 = 480 acres.

21. $A \rightarrow B = \sqrt{3^2 + 4^2} = 5$, so the distance back and forth = 10 miles

22. (300-20)(60)(8) = 134,400 gallons

23. Total surface area = (2)(100')(10') + (2)(40')(10') = 2800 sq.ft.
    Let x = number of gallons. Then, 2.5/100 = x/2800 Solving, x = 70

24. 186°41'22" ÷ 4 = 672,082" ÷ 4 = 168,020.5" ≈ 46.672° ≈ 46°40'19", closest to 46°40'20.5"

25. Each side = $\sqrt{57{,}600 \text{ sq.ft.}} = 240$ ft.
    Perimeter = (4)(240) = 960 ft.

EXAMINATION SECTION
TEST 1

DIRECTIONS: Each question or incomplete statement is followed by several suggested answers or completions. Select the one that BEST answers the question or completes the statement. *PRINT THE LETTER OF THE CORRECT ANSWER IN THE SPACE AT THE RIGHT.*

1. The heat energy required to evaporate 34.5 pounds of water per hour from and at 212°F is called

    A. the factor of evaporation
    B. mechanical horsepower
    C. boiler horsepower
    D. all of the above

2. The blowdown on a safety valve is the

    A. difference between the opening and closing pressures
    B. amount of steam blown down during its opening
    C. amount of condensation during its opening
    D. all of the above

3. Two safety valves are required on a boiler when the heating surface exceeds _____ square feet.

    A. 400   B. 500   C. 600   D. 700

4. An A.S.M.E. boiler has 750 sq.ft. of heating surface, the boiler is built to operate at 150 pounds pressure, and the safety valve is set to pop at 100 pounds. The first method of feeding water is with a pump.
The SECOND method should be

    A. city water pressure
    B. a pump or injector
    C. an automatic feedwater device
    D. an air lift

5. A battery of ten boilers are operating with a maximum allowable working pressure of 100 pounds. Assuming all steam gauges are correct, one boiler shows 110 pounds with its safety valve blowing. The other boilers 80 pounds.
The problem is MOST likely that the

    A. spring in the safety valve is broken
    B. boiler is generating steam in excess of 100 pounds
    C. stop valve is closed or there is an obstruction in the dry pipe
    D. all of the above

6. Tensile strength is defined as the

    A. ability of a material to withstand pulling apart
    B. ultimate point before breaking under pressure
    C. point where the material breaks under tension
    D. all of the above

7. In a longitudinal drum type water tube boiler, the lower tubes in one drum show signs of overheating.
   The trouble is MOST likely caused by

   A. scale deposits in the douncomers or circulating nipples, restricting the water
   B. low water level
   C. too much furnace heat
   D. flames licking

8. Internal corrosion or pitting in a boiler is caused by

   A. acid water
   B. organic matter in the feedwater
   C. corrosive scale
   D. all of the above

9. A heat exchange device consisting of tubes connected to headers and usually placed in the conversion area of boilers is a(n)

   A. air preheater   B. economizer
   C. superheater   D. all of the

10. A vibrating steam line attached to a boiler can cause

    A. fatigue leading to fracture or failure of the valve or connection to which the steam line is attached
    B. cracks In the boiler shell
    C. cracks in the furnace setting
    D. all of the above

11. Heat loss frequently occurs in steam boilers through

    A. air leakage
    B. excessive draft and gases leaving the boiler at high temperature
    C. uncovered or inefficiently covered shell and steam pipes
    D. all of the above

12. The basic principle of the draft gauge rests upon the

    A. venturi tube
    B. Bourdon gauge
    C. response of water in a U-tube to changes In draft pressure
    D. all of the above

13. A modification of the basic U-tube principle to permit easier readings of small changes in draft pressure led to the

    A. vacuum gauge   B. Inclined tube
    C. rectangular gauge   D. all of the avove

14. The Hays pointer gauge is termed a

    A. dry type
    B. diaphragm type
    C. non-liquid draft gauge
    D. all of the above

15. You are having combustion problems with one of your boilers that is not connected to the automatic analyzing section of your plant.
    Which of the following apparatus would you select in order to make a diagnosis?

    A. Tallow candles and a flue gas analyzer
    B. A sensitive differential draft gauge
    C. A high temperature thermometer or pyrometer
    D. All of the above

16. In the operation of a boiler plant, the elements that must be regulated are

    A. fuel supply in proportion to steam demand
    B. air supply
    C. ratio of air to fuel supply
    D. all of the above

17. A theoretically perfect CO_2 reading for fuel oil is 20.9%.
    The LOWEST acceptable percentage for good operation is

    A. 9-12   B. 13-14   C. 15-16   D. 17-18

18. If a furnace is panting or pulsating, the FIRST step to take is to raise the

    A. air supply
    B. fuel supply
    C. oil temperature
    D. all of the above

19. When the speed of burning, or flame propagation in a gas furnace EXCEEDS that of the gas issuing from the port, the flame

    A. grows larger and becomes bright orange
    B. becomes longer turns pale blue
    C. flashes back into the mixing tube
    D. all of the above

20. To prevent furnace accidents, the

    A. furnace must be purged properly before lighting
    B. furnace draft must be closed off
    C. burner must be lit from the fire walls
    D. all of the above

21. The weakness of natural draft is that it depends on many variables, such as the temperature of the atmosphere, height of the stack, direction in which the wind blows, etc.
    To improve draft by lessening these variables,

    A. make the stack higher
    B. install an air preheater
    C. install forced and/or induced draft
    D. all of the above

22. Which of the following can be classified as heat engines? 22.____

    A. Steam engines
    B. Steam and gas turbines
    C. Internal combustion engines
    D. All of the above

23. In many mechanical applications, it is necessary to convert straight line or reciprocating 23.____
    motion to rotating circular motion.
    The MOST efficient machine devised to perform this conversion is the

    A. piston
    B. slide valve
    C. connecting rod and crank
    D. all of the above

24. When a reciprocating engine Is in operation, TOP DEAD CENTER (TDC) and BOTTOM 24.____
    DEAD CENTER (BDC) are overcome with the use of the

    A. slide valve   B. piston
    C. fly wheel   D. all of the

25. An engine in which the speed is kept constant by a governor mounted on the crank shaft 25.____
    placed in one of the band wheels, is called a(n) _____ engine.

    A. compound   B. automatic   C. Corliss   D. gas

26. On a steam engine indicator card, the diagram length is 5.81 Inches, the spring scale is 26.____
    50 pounds per square inch, and the average diagram height is .96 inches.
    The card mean Effective Pressure (MID) is _____ pounds per square inch,

    A. 12.9   B. 20,9   C. 48   D. 209

27. Turbines are erroneously classed as 27.____

    A. impulse and reaction
    B. high pressure and low pressure
    C. high speed and low speed
    D. all of the above

28. When the steam enters near the center of the turbine, and escapes toward the circumfer- 28.____
    ence, the flow is classed as

    A. parallel   B. radial
    C. axial   D. paradoxical

29. To insure safety in operation of a steam turbine, it must be assured that the 29.____

    A. main and emergency governors be tested to see that they are operating satisfactorily
    B. vacuum valve is in good working order
    C. atmospheric relief valve is in good working condition
    D. all of the above

30. In starting a turbine, it must be warmed-up SLOWLY by

    A. admitting steam by slightly opening the stop valve
    B. using electrical pre-heaters
    C. circulating hot oil through the system
    D. all of the above

31. If a turbine speed increases about 10% over its normal speed, a small centrifugal governor releases a trigger arrangement which closes the throttle valve.
    This device is known as a(n)

    A. governor
    B. speed control
    C. overspeed trip
    D. speed sensitive device

32. The type of blading used for gas turbines is

    A. symmetrical
    B. non-symmetrical
    C. expansion
    D. all of the above

33. When taking over the watch in a diesel plant, you check the lube, fuel and cooling pressures, lube discharge, cooling discharge temperature, governor-oil level, crankcase oil level, shaft revolutions, examine the instrument readings on the control board, and look over the log sheet.
    An IMPORTANT item missed was the

    A. lube oil viscosity
    B. pH of the water
    C. cylinder temperature
    D. floor temperature

34. If a diesel engine is running away, you should

    A. cut off the air and fuel supply
    B. check the governor control mechanism
    C. not worry about it; the overspeed trip will take over
    D. all of the above

35. The following type of compressor used for gas turbines is the

    A. axial
    B. centrifugal
    C. combined axial-centrifugal
    D. all of the above

36. The MOST important caution areas around a jet engine are at the

    A. inlet and exhaust
    B. shaft coupling and fuel nozzle
    C. compressor and turbine
    D. all of the above

37. A pump is said to have a flooded suction when

    A. a pump is capable of lifting water
    B. a partial vacuum is created in the pump and suction pipe
    C. water flows into the pump by gravity
    D. all of the above

38. A boiler room has three reciprocating-type pumps.
    In the boiler feedwater pump,

    A. both cylinders are the same diameter
    B. the diameter of the steam cylinder is smaller than that of the water cylinder
    C. the diameter of the steam cylinder is larger than that of the water cylinder
    D. none of the above

39. An injector will NOT start if the steam pressure is *below* _____ lbs.

    A. 40   B. 50   C. 60   D. 80

40. The LOWEST temperature allowed for water entering a boiler is _____ degrees.

    A. 70   B. 90   C. 120   D. 200

41. In starting a boiler feed pump connected to a closed feedwater heater with no exhaust steam entering the heater, you open the drain and observe a flow of continuous water. This is an indication that

    A. everything is in order
    B. the steam trap is working
    C. there is a cracked or leaking tube or coil
    D. all of the above

42. A single pipe heating system is a system

    A. that has a pipe leaving and returning to the boiler
    B. where the condensed water returns through the pipe in which the steam rises
    C. used for hot water only
    D. all of the above

43. Moisture in the atmosphere affects water by

    A. *diminishing* its weight per cubic foot, thus making it more buoyant
    B. *increasing* its capacity for heat, making it more effective for either heating or cooling purposes
    C. *reducing* the amount of oxygen contained in a cubic foot, thus diminishing its value in respiration
    D. all of the above

44. The Copes feedwater regulator is a _____ type.

    A. thermostatic mechanical   B. thermostatic hydraulic
    C. float control   D. all of the above

45. The CORRECT installation of a reducing valve requires that

    A. there must be a by-pass around the valves
    B. a steam gauge be installed on the low pressure side
    C. a relief valve be installed on the low pressure side
    D. all of the above

46. A bucket type steam trap has ceased to operate.　　　　　　　　　　　　　　　　46._____
    It is POSSIBLE that there is a(n)

    A. hole in the bucket
    B. accumulation of mud or scale
    C. accumulation of heavy oil
    D. all of the above

47. Heat energy is ALWAYS　　　　　　　　　　　　　　　　　　　　　　　　　　　　　47._____

    A. potential　　　B. kinetic　　　C. atomic　　　D. mechanical

48. A Prony brake is a　　　　　　　　　　　　　　　　　　　　　　　　　　　　　　　48._____

    A. device for measuring power
    B. device for measuring negative acceleration
    C. tachometer for measuring revolutions per minute
    D. dynamometer

49. In ordering a thrust bearing to support a heavy load, the BEST type would be　　49._____

    A. a babbit-lined sleeve bearing
    B. ball bearings in a specially designed outer race
    C. a roller bearing with modified cone-shaped rollers
    D. a roller bearing with cylindrical rollers

50. The volume of a given quantity of gas will be *increased* MOST if its　　　　　　　50._____

    A. temperature is increased and its pressure is decreased
    B. temperature is constant and its pressure is increased
    C. temperature is increased and its pressure is increased
    D. pressure and temperature are decreased

KEY (CORRECT ANSWERS)

1. C	11. D	21. C	31. C	41. C
2. A	12. C	22. D	32. D	42. B
3. B	13. B	23. C	33. C	43. D
4. B	14. D	24. C	34. A	44. A
5. C	15. D	25. B	35. D	45. D
6. D	16. D	26. C	36. A	46. D
7. A	17. B	27. A	37. C	47. B
8. D	18. A	28. B	38. C	48. A
9. C	19. C	29. D	39. A	49. C
10. A	20. A	30. A	40. B	50. A

TEST 2

DIRECTIONS: Each question or incomplete statement is followed by several suggested answers or completions. Select the one that BEST answers the question or completes the statement. *PRINT THE LETTER OF THE CORRECT ASSWER IN THE SPACE AT THE RIGHT.*

1. A bimetallic element is an essential component of NEARLY all   1.____

   A. optical pyrometers
   B. thermocouples
   C. thermostats
   D. thermels

2. Boiling occurs when   2.____

   A. any liquid attains a temperature of 212°F
   B. the critical temperature of a liquid is reached
   C. surface tension of a liquid is reduced to zero
   D. the vapor pressure of a liquid equals the atmospheric pressure above the liquid

3. Human comfort is MOST closely associated with   3.____

   A. temperature and relative humidity of the air
   B. carbon dioxide content of the air
   C. temperature and specific humidity of the air
   D. heat content and dew point of the air

4. An air conditioning cooling coil is actually the _____ of a refrigeration system.   4.____

   A. evaporator
   B. condenser
   C. expansion valve
   D. liquid received

5. In a typical commercial refrigeration system such as a cold storage warehouse or a walk-in freezer locker, the thermostat in the cooled spaces controls the action of the   5.____

   A. compressor motor starter switch
   B. high pressure cut-out switch
   C. solenoid valve in the liquid refrigerant line
   D. all of the above

6. A foot candle is a measure of   6.____

   A. intensity of illumination on a surface
   B. candle power of a light source
   C. power emitted by a source of light
   D. heat energy received from a standard candle

7. White ceiling and walls aid in Illumination of a room because of   7.____

   A. refraction
   B. absorption
   C. polarization
   D. diffused reflection

8. Which of the following is a measure of the time rate of flow of a quantity of electricity?   8.____

   A. Ampere   B. Coulomb   C. Oersted   D. Kilowatt

9. A wheatstone bridge is USUALLY used for determining 9.____

   A. currents B. potential differences
   C. resistance D. power

10. The volt is the unit used to measure 10.____

    A. potential difference
    B. quantity of electric charge
    C. resistance
    D. current

11. To measure the current being used by a light bulb, it is CORRECT to use a(n) 11.____

    A. watt-meter in series with it
    B. wheatstone bridge
    C. voltmeter in parallel with it
    D. ammeter in series with it

12. House lights are connected in parallel instead of series because 12.____

    A. the voltage must be the same across each lamp
    B. fewer amperes of current will flow through each lamp
    C. the current passing through one lamp will pass through each of the other lamps
    D. the resistance of each lamp is decreased

13. Direct current will NOT operate a(n) 13.____

    A. electric fan B. electromagnet
    C. transformer D. electric toaster

14. The impedance of an AC circuit containing resistance *only* is found by dividing 14.____

    A. amperes by volts B. volts by amperes
    C. coulombs by volts D. henries by volts

15. The CHIEF function of an electric generator in a closed circuit is to 15.____

    A. furnish electrons to the circuit
    B. furnish protons to the circuit
    C. maintain a potential difference
    D. give the electrons their negative charges

16. A direct current generator differs from an alternating current generator in that it has 16.____

    A. a commutator B. slip rings
    C. brushes D. an armature

17. Power companies charge the consumer according to the amount of electrical energy he has used in 17.____

    A. kilowatts B. volts
    C. ampere-hours D. kilowatt-hours

18. A rectifier is a device for changing

    A. electrical energy to mechanical energy
    B. high voltage to low voltage
    C. chemical energy to electrical energy
    D. alternating current to direct current

19. The commercial unit of electrical energy in the United States is

    A. volt-ampere   B. kilowatt
    C. watt-sec   D. kilowatt-hour

20. Electric power produced is USUALLY rated in

    A. kw-hr.   B. amp-sec   C. kva   D. kw

21. The direct current supplied to the field windings of an alternator is called the

    A. wye current   B. exciter current
    C. magnetic current   D. back emf

22. If an Industrial user is causing a low power factor on his lines, the power company will PROBABLY install

    A. ignitrons, to hold the voltage up
    B. indueers, to improve the phase angle
    C. capacitors, to improve phase angle
    D. a larger transformer, to handle the load more efficiently

23. The National Board of Boiler and Pressure Vessel Inspectors is comprised of

    A. the chief inspectors or other officials charged with the enforcement of boilers and pressure vessel with of their jurisdiction
    B. the manufacturers of boilers and pressure vessels
    C. a selected grorp of power engineers
    D. the commissioners from the state departments of labor

24. The PRIMCIPAL objective of the A.S.M.E. code is to

    A. provide minimum standards that will assure reasonable protection to life and property
    B. provide a margin, in construction, for deterioration
    C. assure a reasonably long and safe period of usefulness
    D. all of the above

25. The Uniform Boiler and Pressure Vessel Laws Society, Inc.

    A. recommends the A.S.M.E, Boiler and Pressure Vessel Code as the standard for construction
    B. tries to secure uniform rules and regulations among states, cities, and countries
    C. believes that all laws, rules, and regulations should follow nationally accepted codes and standards
    D. all of the above

26. An Act *to assure safe and healthful working conditions for working men and women, by authorising enfoTsenent of the standards developed under the Act, by assisting and enaouyaging the States in their efforts to assure safe and healthful working conditions* is known as

    A. The Occupational Safety and Health Act
    B. Public Law 91-596
    C. The Williams-Steiger Occupational Safety and Health Act
    D. all of the above

27. Freon is DANGEROUS because

    A. it displaces the oxygen in human body
    B. it decomposes into toxic products
    C. when exposed to a flame or hot surface about 1000°F it decomposes into products that are irritating and poisonous
    D. all of the above

28. Carbon tetrachlorlde CANNOT be used as a cleaning solvent because

    A. it evaporates rapidly and has a very toxic vapor
    B. the vapors rapidly overcome a worker
    C. it can harm the skin and vital body organs
    D. all of the above

29. What safety rule must every engineer and maintenance man know before working on machinery?

    A. Have a work order
    B. Lock the controls in off position with your own padlock
    C. Pull the switch
    D. Wear safety gloves

30. Assume that a fellow worker is in contact with an electrically changed wire.
    Of the following, the BAST reason for NOT grasping the victim's clothing with your bare hands in order to pull him off the wire is that

    A. his clothing may be damp with perspiration
    B. his clothing may be 100% wool
    C. you may be standing on a dry surface
    D. you may be wearing rubber-soled shoes

31. The use of the wrong lubricating oil in an air compressor can result in a breakdoun of the oil causing carbon deposit and a gas (CO).
    All that is needed for an explosion is

    A. a defective unloader   B. a dirty Intercooler
    C. ignition   D. frozen safety valve

32. Non-condeasables in a refrigeration system will

    A. *increase* water usage
    B. *lower* suction pressure
    C. *inarease* current draw of compressor
    D. all of the above

33. Bubbles in the liquid line sight glass of a refrigeration system could be caused by a(n)

    A. overcharge of oil
    B. leaking discharge valves in the compressor
    C. bad low pressure switch
    D. plugged drier

34. The causes of reduced condenser air quantity are
    I. dirty fan blades
    II. dirt on coil
    III. prevailing winds
    IV. lack of freon
The CORRECT answer is:

    A. I, II
    B. II, III
    C. I, II, III
    D. II, III, IV

35. High suction pressure and low head pressure indicate the compressor is deficient in

    A. refrigerant gas
    B. pumping capacity
    C. oil charge
    D. size

36. Solenoid valves may hum due to

    A. low voltage
    B. a loose connection
    C. sticking plunger
    D. all of the above

37. The cost of operating an air conditioning plant is $320 a day for 100 days $435 a day for 265 days.
what is the total annual cost for operating this plant?

    A. $300,000   B. $208,096   C. $147,275   D. $128,200

38. A power plant uses 70,000 gallons of No. 6 fuel oil per seven day week. How many gallons would be used in one day?

    A. 10,000   B. 7,000   C. 6,000   D. 3,500

39. Air contains 23 parts of oxygen and 77 parts of nitrogen approximately. what is the weight of the oxygen in 12 pounds of air?

    A. 12   B. 9.24   C. 2.76   D. 1.54

40. What is the area of a piston 7 inches in diameter?

    A. 70   B. 38.5   C. 32.2   D. 25.7

41. An engine has an Indicated horsepower of 31 and a brake horsepower of 27.466. what is its mechanical efficiency, usng the formula $M = \dfrac{Hn}{Hi}$

    A. 60%   B. 75.5%   C. 88.6%   D. 92.5%

42. A boiler requires 30,000 pounds of water per hour.
    What size of feedpipe, in inches, is necessary if the rate is 360 feet per minute, using the formula $d = \sqrt{\dfrac{1830}{v}}$?

    A. 1   B. 2   C. 4   D. 6

43. A 200 H.P. package boiler operating on No, 5 oil uses 0.280 gallons per BHP per hour. If this boiler operates continuously at full capacity and 80% efficiency, how many gallons of fuel will this boiler use per a 24 hour day?

    A. 2,058   B. 1,562   C. 1,344   D. 1,228

44. A power plant has a total of 235 horsepower in electric motors.
    How many kilowatt hours does this amount to if motors run 10 hours per day, using the formula 1 horsepower = 746 watt hours?

    A. 1,753   B. 17,531   C. 175,310   D. 1,753,100

45. A steam turbine turns at 3600 RPM and the diameter of Its largest rotor is 12 ft.
    Find the linear velocity of a point on the tip of a rotor blade in ft/sec?

    A. 4200   B. 3600   C. 2260   D. 1200

46. In an alternating current circuit, the voltmeter and ammeter readings are 110 and 20, respectively.
    What is the apparent power?

    A. 2,200 watts   B. 4,400 watts
    C. 440 volts   D. 220 volts

47. If the angle oflog in the preceding question is 45°, what is the true power? (cos 45° = .707)

    A. 220 volts   B. 1000 watts
    C. 1555.4   D. 440 volts

48. An ice plant freezes ice in 300lb. blocks from water at 70°F. Each block is frozen in a galvanized steel *can* (specific head of steel = 0.115), whose weight is 120 lbs. The ice is at 10°F when the process is complete.
    How many BTU's of cooling capacity are required to produce each 300 lb. block of ice?

    A. 580   B. 5,873   C. 58,730   D. 587,300

49. A cast Iron water pipe with an 8 Inch Inside diameter is to be subjected to an Internal pressure of 200 pounds per square inch.
    What should the MINIMUM thickness of the pipe be, in inches, so that the stress does NOT exceed 3,500 pounds per square inch, using the formula S = Pr/t?
    _____ inch.

    A. .228   B. .500   C. .728   D. .750

50. A plain butt weld joins two steel plates, which are each 1/2 inch thick and 8 inches wide. 50.____
The allowable working stress is 13,000 pounds per square inch for a tensile loading of such a welded joint.
What is the ALLOWABLE tensile load, in pounds, that may be applied to the plates, using the formula P = SWbt?

   A. 40,000   B. 52,000   C. 60,000   D. 65,000

KEY (CORRECT ANSWERS)

1. B	11. D	21. B	31. C	41. C
2. D	12. A	22. C	32. D	42. B
3. A	13. C	23. A	33. D	43. C
4. A	14. B	24. D	34. C	44. A
5. C	15. C	25. D	35. B	45. C
6. A	16. A	26. D	36. D	46. A
7. D	17. D	27. D	37. C	47. C
8. A	18. D	28. D	38. A	48. C
9. C	19. D	29. B	39. C	49. A
10. A	20. C	30. A	40. B	50. B

THEORY OF HEAT

CONTENTS

	Page
A. INTRODUCTION	1
B. MEASUREMENT OF HEAT	1
C. KINDS OF HEAT	2
D. PRESSURE	4
E. VAPORIZATION	6
F. PHYSICAL CONDITIONS OF VAPORS AND LIQUIDS	7
G. EXPANSION AND CONTRACTION OF SUBSTANCE	7
H. HEAT TRANSFER	8
I. INSULATION	9

THEORY OF HEAT

A. INTRODUCTION

A1. General.—As mentioned earlier, heat is a very relative term. Usually one thinks of it as a means of warming the body, or some object, to a desired temperature. Strange as it may seem, heat is ever present, even in a block of ice. In this chapter, heat is explained in terms of how it is used and transferred from substance to substance. Heat transfer is what all refrigeration systems are designed to accomplish. To understand the basic principles of refrigeration, it is most important that the student have a definite understanding of the relationship of heat, temperatures, and pressures.

A2. Matter Defined.—Matter is anything that has weight and occupies space. All substances are forms of matter in one of three stages: solid, liquid, or gaseous. An example of a substance in its three stages is water.

In its natural state water is a liquid. It has weight, volume, and takes the shape of the container which holds it. If it is heated in a closed container to its boiling point and more heat is added, it changes to steam or vapor which is its gaseous state. It has weight and occupies the volume or space of the container. When water is frozen, it becomes ice or is in its solid state. In this state, it has weight and volume, and it takes a definite shape.

Theoretically, all substances can be converted from one to another of the three states by the addition or withdrawal of heat. However, chemical compounds differ in the ease or difficulty with which they may be changed from one to another of the three physical states. Some, like water, can very readily be converted into each of the three states; others, like paper, oxidize, or burn, at high temperatures and cannot be converted into all three. Before paper burns, it changes to a gas, but never to a liquid. The science of refrigeration depends upon changes in physical state through heating or cooling.

A3. Definition of Heat.—Heat is a form of energy. It cannot be seen or shaped, nor can it be created or destroyed. It can only be transferred from substance to substance.

All substances are made up of tiny molecules. These molecules are in constant motion and moving against each other. As the temperature of these molecules increases, so does their activity, and as heat is taken away their activity and temperature decrease. If all heat is extracted from a substance (absolute zero temperature), the molecular motion will become dormant.

B. MEASUREMENT OF HEAT

B1. Intensity and Quantity.—From experience we know that heat and temperature are related. If heat is added to a substance the temperature of the substance will rise, and if heat is taken away the temperature will decrease. There is a difference, however, in quantity and intensity. Heat is measured (1) by its intensity, and (2) by the quantity of it possessed by a substance. This is readily understood by comparing a spoonful of hot water with a pailful of warm water. The hot water in the spoon has a greater intensity of heat, but the warm water in the pail possesses a larger quantity of heat, though at a lower intensity.

B2. Thermometer.—Intensity of heat is measured by the ordinary thermometer with which everyone is familiar. The two methods of dividing and numbering the thermometer scales in common use are the Fahrenheit and the Centigrade. Another scale not so common but used by scientists is the Kelvin.

B3. Fahrenheit Scale.—The temperature scale most commonly used in refrigeration is the Fahrenheit scale represented by the designator °F. This scale is fixed to divide the

THEORY OF HEAT

difference between melting ice and boiling water into 180 equal degrees. The melting ice is represented by a mark of 32° F, and boiling water at 212° F. Degrees above and below these are also equal divisions shown on the scale. When reaching the temperature where all molecular action in all substances ceases, a thermometer reading of -459.69° F would be indicated. This is called absolute zero. Scientists have been able, under controlled conditions, to measure temperatures within a few thousandths of absolute zero.

B4. **Centigrade Scale.**—The centigrade thermometer is scaled in degrees and indicated by °C. On this scale, ice melts at 0° C and water boils at 100° C. The 100 degrees between melting point and boiling point are equally divided on the scale. The absolute zero temperature on the centigrade scale is -273.16° C.

The centigrade scaled thermometer is used in most countries except the United States and Britain. It is used universally in scientific work.

B5. **Absolute or Kelvin Scale.**—The Kelvin scale is graduated in degrees starting at zero. On this scale, 0° K is equal to -273° C or -460° F, or absolute zero. The boiling point of water, 373° K, and the melting point of ice, 273° K, are equal to readings on the Fahrenheit and centigrade scales as shown in figure 1.

B6. **British Thermal Unit.**—The quantity of heat possessed by a substance is measured in terms of the British thermal unit, abbreviated Btu. A Btu is the quantity of heat required to raise the temperature of one pound of pure water one degree Fahrenheit at or near 39.10° F. This is the temperature at which water is at maximum density. For example, to raise the temperature of five pounds of water from 39° to 49° F, or from 160° to 170° F, requires $5 \times 10 = 50$ Btu. For all practical purposes, the Btu is considered constant between 32° and 212° F, though it does vary a slight amount.

C. KINDS OF HEAT

C1. **General.**—To have an understanding of the terminology used in refrigeration and air conditioning, it is essential that the meaning of the terms discussed in this section be known. Some terms seem closely related, but the meaning and way they are applied is very important. The terms considered here apply to heat.

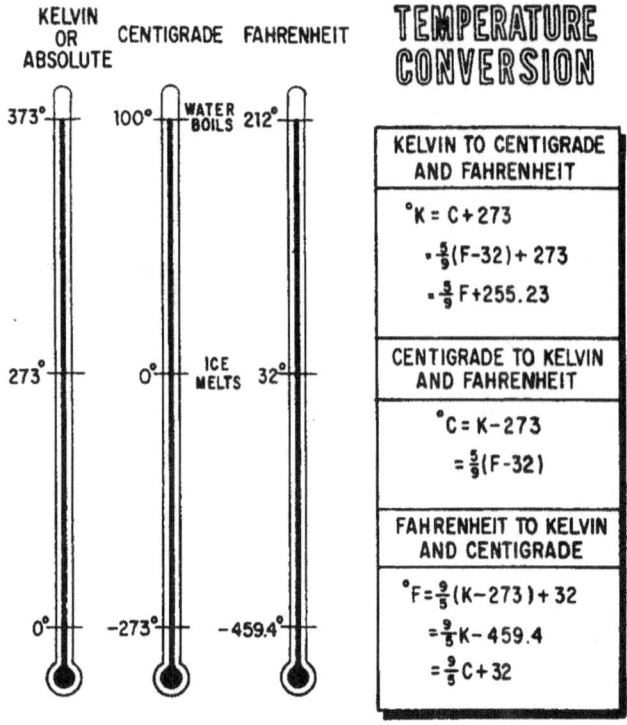

Figure 1.—Comparison of Fahrenheit, centigrade, and Kelvin temperature scales.

C2. **Specific Heat.**—Specific heat is the number of Btu that must be added to a unit weight of substance to raise its temperature 1 degree Fahrenheit. Since most substances held to a constant weight vary in volume, varying numbers of Btu are required to change the temperature 1 degree Fahrenheit per unit.

Technically, the specific heat of a substance is the ratio of the amount of heat required to change the temperature of a unit weight of that substance 1 degree to the amount of heat required to change the temperature of the same weight of water one degree. Since the specific heat of water is, by definition, equal to 1, the specific heat of other substances are expressed as decimals. Examples of the specific heat of some substances follow:

Material	Specific Heat (Btu/Lb)
Wood	.327
Ice	.504
Iron	.129
Copper	.095
Glass	.187

Mercury	.033
Alcohol	.615
Liquid Ammonia at 40° F.	1.100

C3. **Thermal Capacity.**—Thermal capacity is closely related to specific heat. The specific heat of a substance is the number of Btu necessary to raise the temperature of one pound of the substance one degree Fahrenheit. The thermal capacity of a substance is the amount of heat required to raise the temperature of its whole mass one degree. Hence, thermal capacity equals the specific heat of a substance multiplied by its mass. Thermal capacity may be said to express the total capacity of a given quantity of a substance for absorbing and storing heat. Thermal capacity is stated, not as a ratio, but as a certain number of Btu.

C4. **Sensible Heat.**—Heat that is added to, or subtracted from, a substance that changes its temperature but not its physical state is called sensible heat. It is the heat that can be indicated on a thermometer. This is the heat which human senses also can react to, at least within certain ranges. For example, if a person puts his finger into a cup of water, his senses readily tell him whether it is cold, cool, tepid, hot, or very hot. Human senses are not sufficiently discriminating to give precise information about the extreme temperatures of ice and steam or other substances having temperatures beyond the range of human sensory mechanisms. Ice merely seems cold and steam seems hot whatever their temperatures. Sensible heat is applied to a solid (as ice), a liquid (as water), or a vapor/gas (as steam) as indicated on a thermometer. The term sensible heat does not apply to the process of conversion from one physical state to another.

C5. **Latent Heat.**—Heat absorbed, or given up, during the conversion of a substance from one physical state to another has another name. This is called latent heat. The term, latent heat, has two forms; latent heat of fusion and latent heat of vaporization.

Latent is taken from the Greek language meaning hidden. When latent heat is added to or subtracted from a substance, and the physical change takes place, there is no change in the sensible heat or temperature of the substance.

C6. **Latent Heat of Fusion.**—If heat is applied to a piece of ice at a temperature of 0° F, the temperature of the ice would gradually rise. This change in temperature, which can be indicated by placing a thermometer on the ice, is called sensible heat as stated previously. No change in state takes place, only a change in the temperature of the ice.

As more sensible heat is added, the temperature of the ice finally reaches 32° F. Now, as more heat is absorbed by the ice, the ice melts or changes state, but the temperature of the liquid is also 32° F. The heat added during the process of melting the ice at 32° to water at 32° F (at sea level barometric pressure) is the hidden or latent heat of fusion.

This process also works in the reverse order. When water is chilled to 32° F and more heat is taken away to form it into ice at 32° F, this heat is also latent heat of fusion.

Here is where one of the most important laws in physics is involved in refrigeration; heat can never be destroyed. It can only be transferred from one substance to another. So, the same amount of heat required to melt the ice into water must be removed from the water to convert it back to ice.

The latent heat of fusion for pure water at 32° F and at sea-level barometric pressure is 143.33 Btu per pound.

C7. **Latent Heat of Vaporization.**—As the last of the ice melts, the temperature of the water begins to rise. The temperature causing the rise is sensible heat. When the temperature of water reaches 212° F, the temperature stops rising and another change takes place. More heat is added and the water boils or changes to steam, but there is no change in temperature. This too is hidden heat. As the last of the water vaporizes and more heat is added, the temperature will again rise and again we are dealing with sensible heat.

The heat added to, or taken away, in the process of changing water to steam vapor, or from vapor/steam back to water, is called latent heat of vaporization. All substances that change from liquid to a vapor or gas go through this stage.

The value set for one pound of water at 212° F to be converted into steam, or steam converted to water, is 970.4 Btu. Other changes of state with variation of temperature, and the number of Btu required by such changes for a pound of water, are shown in figure 2.

THEORY OF HEAT

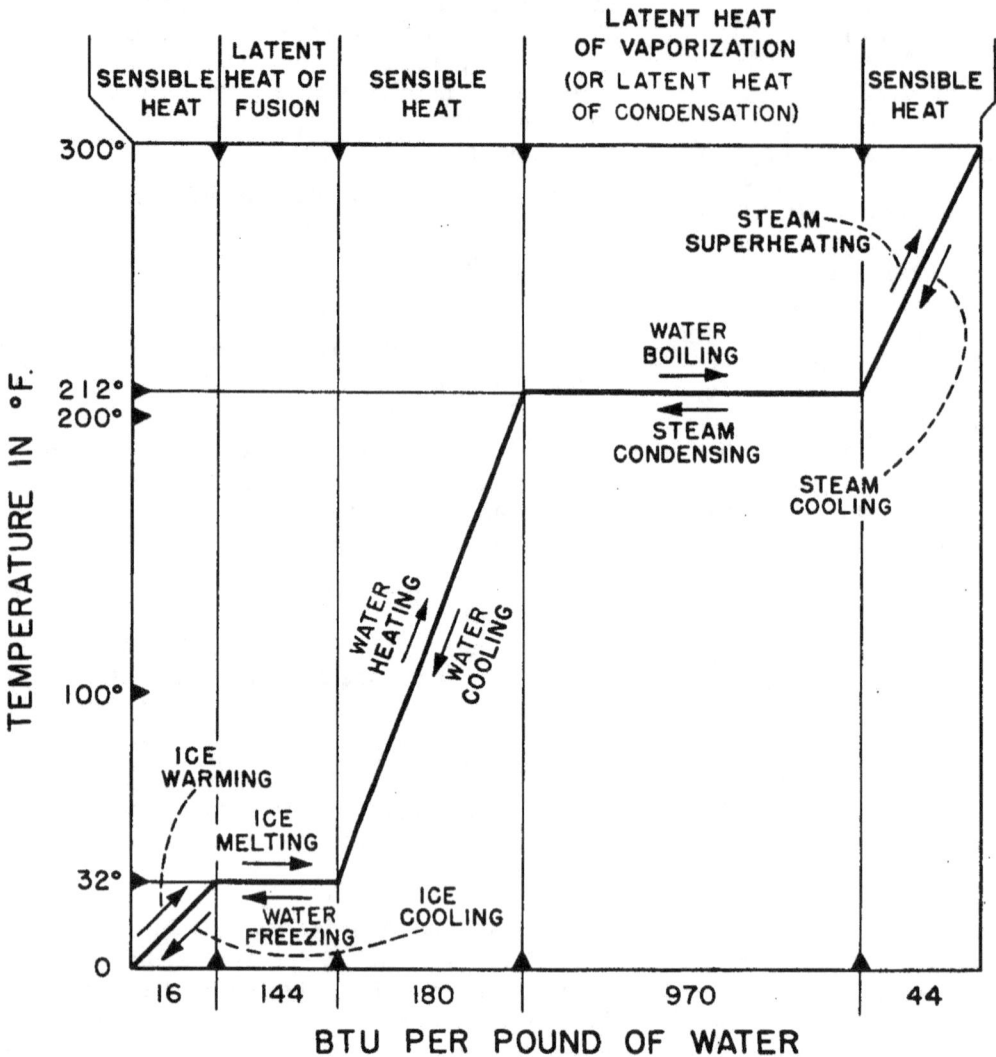

Figure 2.—Relationship between sensible heat and latent heat for water at atmospheric pressure.

C8. Total Heat.—The term total heat is used with two different meanings and care must be used in reading textbooks in order that the meaning intended is properly understood. These two usages are as follows:

Strictly speaking, the total heat of a substance is the total heat energy calculated from absolute zero in Btu. It is specific heat x mass x absolute temperature. Since there is no instrument, however, for measuring heat directly on the absolute scale, and since it would also require high numbers, other starting points are arbitrarily chosen. For the liquid water, the arbitrary starting point is 32° F.

In refrigeration and air conditioning, the total heat of a substance or of the air in a room is all the heat present, that is:

Total Heat = Sensible Heat + Latent Heat

In discussions, the term heat content is sometimes used. This term has the same meaning as total heat.

D. PRESSURE

D1. Atmospheric Pressure.—At the beginning of this chapter, we defined matter as nything which occupies space and has weight. As air is matter, it too has weight. The weight of this air is called atmospheric pressure. The valued scale for a column of air 1 inch square in cross-sectional area at the base and reaching from sea level to the upper limit of the earth's atmosphere at 32° F and at sea level is 14.696 pounds. This will vary due to condition changes in the air above the earth. For all practical purposes, the value is considered to be 14.7 pounds per square inch (psi) at sea level.

D2. Mercury Barometer.—To measure atmospheric pressure, scientists have developed a simple instrument called a mercury barometer. It is constructed with a glass tube that is a little over thirty inches long and sealed at one end. The tube is then completely filled with mercury. By placing a finger over the open end and inverting into an open dish of mercury, the mercury column in the tube will fall, leaving a vacuum in the space above the mercury. The air pressure exerted on the surface of the mercury in the dish will maintain a column of mercury in the tube equal to the pressure on the surface. At sea level pressure of 14.7 psi, the height of the column of mercury in the tube will be 29.921 inches. As atmospheric pressure is increased or decreased, the height of the mercury column will vary in relation to the pressure.

D3. Aneroid Barometer.—Another device used to measure atmospheric pressure is the aneroid barometer. This type is more compact and easier to handle than the mercury barometer, but not as accurate.

The aneroid barometer consists of an airtight metal box, with a partial vacuum inside, and a flexible side that can move slightly under varying pressures. The motion of the flexible side is transmitted through gears and levers to a pointer that is calibrated to a scale on the dial. This scale is graduated in inches and corresponds to the inches of mercury in the mercury barometer.

A good aneroid barometer will show a slight increase in pressure when lowered from a table to the floor.

D4. Conversion of Barometer Readings.—Since the aneroid and mercury barometers indicate the atmospheric pressure in inches, a conversion factor must be used to convert this pressure to pounds per square inch. At an air temperature of 32° F and at mean sea level, the mercury column stands at 29.921 inches and corresponds to a pressure of 14.696 psi. By dividing 14.696 by 29.921, the result will give the conversion factor of 0.491. To convert the reading on the barometer, multiply the reading by the conversion factor.

D5. Variation of Pressure and Boiling Point with Altitude.—The pressures and boiling points of substances will vary with altitudes. If an uncovered container filled with fresh water at mean sea level is heated until the water boils, a thermometer inserted in the water shows that its temperature is 212° F, and a barometer shows that the atmospheric pressure is approximately 14.7 psi. However, if the pot of boiling water is on a hilltop 1000 feet above sea level, the thermometer shows that the water boils at 210° F when the barometer reads approximately 14.14 psi. Similar variations in boiling point and barometric pressure are observed at different altitudes, as indicated in the following table:

Feet above sea level	Pressure (psi)	Boiling point of Water (°F)
Sea level	14.70	212
2000	13.57	208
4000	12.49	204
6000	11.54	200
8000	10.62	196

D6. Pressure-Temperature Relationship for Change of State.—It is not variations of pressure and temperatures at different altitudes to which special attention is directed, but the relationship between the temperature of vaporization and the corresponding pressure. It is not necessary, however, to go to different heights to obtain different pressures; different pressures may be obtained by mechanical means at any location.

For example, a boiling liquid and its vapor may be contained in an airtight metal cylinder with a piston. By moving the piston in or out, the pressure within may be increased or decreased. If the piston is pushed in, thus increasing the pressure inside, a thermometer shows that the change of state from liquid to vapor requires a temperature higher than 212° F. If the piston is pulled out, thus decreasing the pressure within, the thermometer shows that the change of state from liquid to vapor takes place at a temperature lower than 212° F. Many types of such mechanical arrangements are in common use.

This relationship of vaporization temperature and pressure, which varies for different substances, follows an exact law, and may be tabulated accurately for each substance.

D7. Pressure Gage.—Pressures within an airtight system of pipes, tanks, and cylinders are usually measured by a Bourdon-tube pressure gage. In this gage there is a small tube, flattened (not round) in cross-section, and curved to about three-quarters of a circle. One end of this curved tube is firmly fixed to the mounting, or case; the other end is free and slightly movable. A delicate lever system which turns a pointer on a circular scale is attached to the free end. The fixed end of this tube is joined by connections to the vapor system, and made part of that system. Increases in vapor pressure tend to straighten the curved tube, thus rotating the pointer. The scale is marked to indicate the pressure values in units of pounds per square inch.

The scale on the Bourdon-tube pressure gage is marked with zero to correspond to standard atmospheric pressure. Consequently, zero gage pressure equals 14.7 pounds per square inch. When the pressure of the vapor inside the curved tube is 14.7 psi, it is equal to the atmospheric pressure outside the tube, and there is no tendency for the curved tube to straighten. Hence, this pressure is taken as the zero point on the gage.

D8. Gage Pressure.—The pressure indicated by a Bourdon-tube pressure gage is in reality the difference between the vapor pressure inside and the air pressure outside the curved tube. Readings from such a gage are always designated _gage pressure_.

Gage pressure is expressed in pounds per square inch. For convenience, this term is indicated by its abbreviated form psi. Often, where the meaning is unmistakable, the word _pounds_ alone is used; for example, 20 pounds' pressure means 20 pounds per square inch pressure.

D9. Absolute Pressure.—The term _absolute pressure_ is used to designate the true total pressure inside the enclosed vapor system. Suppose the pressure gage stands at 6 pounds. Then, since zero gage pressure means 14.7 pounds inside (to balance 14.7 pounds air pressure outside the tube), the total, or absolute pressure of the vapor is 14.7 pounds plus 6 pounds, or 20.7 pounds. If an accurate knowledge of the pressure is required, the atmospheric pressure, converted from a barometer reading, is used instead of the 14.7-pound standard.

D10. Vacuum or Negative Gage Pressure.—As stated, the standard atmospheric pressure of 14.7 psi is taken as the zero point on the gage. A gage dealing only with increases in pressure has a single scale marked from 0 to 300 pounds, or some other upper limit, and is read in psi gage pressure.

But, pressures may decrease below atmospheric pressure as well as increase. Pressures below 14.7 psi are known as partial vacuums. This term is merely for convenience in referring to pressures below ordinary atmospheric pressure, since such a pressure is far from approaching a vacuum.

A gage that registers pressures lower than standard atmospheric pressure is called a vacuum gage. Such gages are graduated to read in inches of vacuum. Approximately 30 inches of vacuum equal zero pounds absolute pressure.

D11. Compound Gage.—A compound gage is sometimes called a compound pressure and vacuum gage. It has an extended range covering pressures both below and above atmospheric pressure. The scale is graduated to the left and right of zero (atmospheric pressure). Above atmospheric pressure readings are in psi, and below atmospheric pressures are readings of inches of vacuum.

Gages used on the suction side of most refrigeration units are of the compound type.

E. VAPORIZATION

E1. Kinds of Vaporization.—Ebullition, evaporation, and sublimation are the three kinds of vaporization, or methods of converting from one physical state to another.

E2. Ebullition.—Ebullition is the technical term for ordinary boiling. It is a rapid and visible process. By looking into an uncovered container of boiling water, one can see that ebullition, or boiling, is taking place. Starting from the bottom and sides, large and small bubbles rise to the surface and escape from the liquid.

E3. **Evaporation.**—Evaporation is a slow and invisible process which takes place only from the surface of a liquid. Under ordinary conditions, evaporation cannot be seen. Any liquid in an uncovered container will gradually evaporate, its level slowly falling until all liquid is gone. Water continually evaporates from the surface of all open bodies such as rivers, lakes, ponds, and oceans. Wet clothing, hung on a line to dry, does so, by this process.

Since evaporation is a form of vaporization, it results in the removal of latent heat. Therefore, it is a cooling process, though a slow one. When a person goes in swimming on a cool day with a wind blowing, it is the evaporation process that makes him feel uncomfortable, rather than the temperature itself. The human body gets rid of excess heat and moisture naturally and continually by evaporation.

Some liquids evaporate much faster than others. For example, alcohol will evaporate much faster than water.

E4. **Sublimation.**—The third method of converting from one physical state to another is called sublimation. It consists of converting from a solid directly to the vapor state without passing through the intermediate or liquid state. Ice and snow, even when much below the freezing point, slowly disappear without melting. Washed clothes, hung out-of-doors in temperatures below 32° F, first freeze stiff, and then dry soft. Both these phenomena are caused by sublimation.

Sublimation has little application to refrigeration engineering. It has, however, considerable use in the small scale cooling of bottled foods, ice cream, and other food stuffs by the use of solid carbon dioxide, or dry ice, which sublimes to a vapor under atmospheric pressure.

E5. **Vapor and Gas.**—The terms vapor and gas both refer to matter in the physical state that is neither solid or liquid. There is, however, a definite distinction between the two.

Vapor condenses very readily to a liquid state under small changes of temperature or pressure, or both, and constantly does so under ordinary conditions of nature. It may be said to be very close to the liquid state, although it is a vapor.

Gas, on the other hand, exists under ordinary conditions in a gaseous state. To change it to a liquid state, special laboratory apparatus capable of producing extreme changes of pressure is required. A gas may be said to be far removed from the liquid state and cannot change under ordinary natural conditions.

In refrigeration, the word gas is frequently used instead of the more correct term vapor.

F. PHYSICAL CONDITIONS OF VAPORS AND LIQUIDS

F1. **State and Condition.**—The term state is used to refer to the three forms of matter: solid, liquid, and gas or vapor. However, a substance in any one of the three states may be found in different conditions. Hence, the term condition is also used. A vapor ordinarily exists in either of two conditions, as a saturated vapor or as superheated vapor.

F2. **Saturated Vapor.**—The saturated vapor is a vapor at the temperature corresponding to its boiling point at a given pressure. Saturated vapors are classed as either wet or dry. If they contain liquid particles of their substance, they are termed wet. If no particles are present, they are termed dry.

Saturated vapors are usually in the wet state due to the boiling action of the substance. The bubbles, as they break away from the surface as a vapor, will carry tiny droplets of the liquid suspended in the vapor.

F3. **Superheated Vapor.**—If a vapor is not in contact with a boiling liquid, either because the liquid has been converted into vapor or because the vapor has been separated from the boiling liquid, further application of heat produces a rise in temperature of the vapor under the same given pressure. Such a vapor is called superheated vapor.

F4. **Saturation Temperature.**—If a liquid is heated, it finally boils at a temperature that is the result of the pressure present. Such a temperature is called the saturation temperature corresponding to the given pressure. This term is frequently used in air conditioning and means the boiling point, or the condensation point, at the given pressure.

A liquid that is at the saturation temperature corresponding to a given pressure, and is under that pressure, is called a saturated liquid.

G. EXPANSION AND CONTRACTION OF SUBSTANCE

G.1. **General.**—In general, all substances, whether solid, liquid, or gas, decrease in volume when cooled and increase in volume when heated. In gases and vapors, the amount of change is large; in liquids and solids it is small. In all cases, great forces are produced and it is necessary in all engineering construction to allow for the operation of these forces. Different substances vary in the amount of change in volume they undergo for the same differences in temperature.

G2. Expansion and Contraction of Water.—Water contracts as it is cooled until the temperature 39.2°F is reached. At this point the change in volume reverses and if the water is cooled further, the volume increases. When water freezes into ice, an enormous force is brought into play. This force is sufficient to split large rocks, burst iron pipes and even steel tanks, unless provisions are allowed for the expansion.

G3. Expansion and Contraction at the Change of State.—At their melting point, substances follow no general rule regarding expansion and contraction. Some metals like iron, bismuth, and antimony, contract on melting and expand on solidifying; but most others like gold, silver, and copper, expand on melting and contract on solidifying. All liquids, however, expand greatly when changing into a vapor unless constrained mechanically, as in a closed container. An example of this expansion is the large clouds of steam continually rising from a container of boiling water.

G4. Specific Volume.—The specific volume of a substance is a number that indicates the number of cubic feet occupied by one pound of the substance at a given temperature and pressure. Specific volume varies greatly for different substances and for the same substances at different temperatures and pressures.

The specific volume for boiling water at atmospheric pressure is 0.0167 cubic feet per pound, and of steam at the same pressure it is 26.79 cubic feet per pound. Thus, water in changing its state from liquid to vapor at ordinary atmospheric pressure increases in volume 1604 times.

H. HEAT TRANSFER

H1. How Heat is Transferred.—As explained earlier in this chapter, heat can neither be created nor destroyed, but only transferred from one substance to another. This transfer is accomplished through one of three ways: radiation, convection, and conduction.

H2. Radiation.—In radiation, heat is transmitted through empty space (a vacuum), as from the sun to the earth's atmosphere. Heat, light, electricity, radio, and x-rays are all known to be energy in the form of transverse vibrations. Physically, they differ only in their wave lengths, but their physical effects are quite different, as is evident by comparing heat with radio waves. In radiation, nothing but energy really travels.

Radiation does not heat the air through which it passes, it heats only the objects on which it falls. Not only the sun, but other objects such as flames, stoves, electric light bulbs, machines, and the earth itself, radiate heat. Even our bodies radiate heat.

H3. Convection.—Convection is the transfer of heat by the movement of a substance (gas or liquid) through a space. Examples of this include a current of warm air in a room, a current of warm water such as the Gulf Stream, and warm air rising from a hot water or steam radiator.

H4. Conduction.—The transfer of heat from one molecule to another, either of the same substance or of different substances, by direct contact is called conduction. A molecule of a substance is the smallest particle of a substance that retains the special qualities of that substance. Any further subdivision of a molecule separates it into the atoms of which it is composed.

Physical contact is necessary for conduction of heat, and the conduction takes place from the region of the higher temperature to the lower temperature. For example, if a person holds a metal bar of iron in one hand and places the other end of the bar in a fire, the heat passes from the fire to the bar, then along the bar to the hand. Here physical contact is made in each instance; fire to bar, bar to hand.

H5. Thermal Conductance.—Suppose that two bars are held, one of iron and one of copper, of exactly the same size and at the same temperature. If one end of each bar is placed in a fire at the same time, heat will reach the hand holding the copper bar more quickly than through the iron bar. This is because some substances conduct heat more readily than others.

This characteristic of a substance is called its thermal or heat conductance. The low and high thermal conductance of substances is of great importance in refrigeration and air conditioning. Some substances are used for transfer of heat while others are used to prevent heat transfer.

I. INSULATION

11. **Need for Insulation.**—It is comparatively easy to heat or cool articles or enclosed spaces. It is not easy, however, to keep them at a constant temperature because heat constantly tends to flow to the lower temperature areas.

When it is desired to keep a space within a certain temperature range, it is necessary to prevent the transfer of heat to or from the space. Fortunately this can be done, fairly successfully, by the use of a substance with low thermal conductance.

12. **Insulators.**—Poor conductors are good insulators. Poor conductors include such substances as cork, wood, sawdust, paper, brick, rubber, fur, feathers, felt, plastics, cotton, and dead air space. Most solids that are poor conductors are also porous in nature, and the pores or air cells are small in size. Much of the insulating quality results from these tiny pockets.

The "K" conductivity factor for an insulating material is the amount of Btu per square foot, per hour, per °F, that can penetrate the insulation for a thickness of one inch. Some of the more commonly used insulating materials and "K" conductivity factors follow:

Material	"K" Factor
Cork with pitch	0.428
Sawdust, pine	0.57
Wool, pure	0.26
Glass	5.0
Air (dead)	0.175

13. **Low Temperature Insulation.**—The requirements for low-temperature insulation are somewhat different from those for high-temperature insulation. Any water vapor present in the air tends to condense into liquid droplets or film on a cold surface. This is commonly called sweating. This condensed water penetrates a porous material and fills the air cells, lessening its insulating ability. It may freeze there and ice is a very poor insulator of heat. Insulating materials for use with refrigeration systems are manufactured to resist the penetration of moisture, and to be durable under conditions of high humidity.

Low-temperature pipe lines must be thoroughly insulated to prevent heat from entering the refrigerant contained therein. The usual insulation is a cork composition molded into sections that fit snugly around the pipes and fittings. Other materials, such as rock wool and mineral wool, are also used in the same way.

Before applying the covering, all pipes should be carefully cleaned, all rust removed, and dried. If possible, the hangers and braces should be attached around the outside of the insulation to prevent the transfer of heat by conduction and to prevent moisture from entering the insulation.

When molded sections are installed on pipe lines, they should be staggered and all joints should be placed so as to come together at the top and bottom of the pipe. After all seams are sealed, the covering should be painted with an asphalt paint, to make it waterproof.

Always repair ruptured insulation as soon as possible to prevent the entry of moisture. Make sure the pipe is dry and all seams are sealed when making repairs.

www.ingramcontent.com/pod-product-compliance
Lightning Source LLC
Chambersburg PA
CBHW082212300426
44117CB00016B/2769